NOLS
Wilderness Navigation

D1555474

NOLS
Wilderness
Navigation

3rd Edition

Gene Trantham and Darran Wells
Edited by Helen Wilson

STACKPOLE
BOOKS
Guilford, Connecticut

Published by Stackpole Books
An imprint of The Rowman & Littlefield Publishing Group, Inc.
4501 Forbes Blvd., Ste. 200
Lanham, MD 20706
www.rowman.com

Distributed by NATIONAL BOOK NETWORK
800-462-6420

Cover photo by Moe Witschard

All illustrations by Jon Cox except as follows: pp. 2, 115: The National Atlas of the United States of America, United States Department of the Interior Geological Survey, 1970, Courtesy of the University of Texas Libraries, The University of Texas at Austin; p. 3 (top and bottom): iGage; pp. 6, 26 (bottom), 27, 28, 50, 51, 52 (top and bottom), 54, 56, 76: USGS; pp. 11, 35, 63: NOAA; p. 26 (top): © iStock.com/powerofforever; pp. 37, 119, 121, 126: U.S. Geological Survey/Caroline Stover; p. 60: © iStock.com/Wittayayut; pp. 124–25: Denis J. Dean, professor of geospatial science, Colorado State University; p. 173: © iStock.com/JohnDWilliams

British Library Cataloguing in Publication Information available

Library of Congress Cataloging-in-Publication Data

Names: Trantham, Gene S. (Gene Starr), 1962- author. | Wells, Darran, author.
 | NOLS
Title: NOLS wilderness navigation / Gene Trantham and Darran Wells, edited by
 Helen Wilson.
Description: Third Edition. | Guilford, Connecticut : Stackpole Books, [2018]
 | Second edition: Mechanicsburg, Pennsylvania : Stackpole Books, 2013, by
 Darran Wells. |"Distributed by NATIONAL BOOK NETWORK"—T.p. verso. |
 Includes bibliographical references and index.
Identifiers: LCCN 2018016756 (print) | LCCN 2018017076 (ebook) | ISBN
 9780811767682 (e-book) | ISBN 9780811737739 (paperback)
Subjects: LCSH: Orienteering—Equipment and supplies. | Navigation—Equipment
 and supplies. | Outdoor recreation—Equipment and supplies.
Classification: LCC GV200.4 (ebook) | LCC GV200.4 .W45 2018 (print) | DDC
 796.58—dc23
LC record available at https://lccn.loc.gov/2018016756

FSC
www.fsc.org
MIX
Paper from
responsible sources
FSC® C008955

NOLS books are printed by FSC® certified printers. The Forest Stewardship Council™ encourages responsible management of the world's forests.

Printed in the United States of America

Contents

Acknowledgments

My path to the outdoors, and specifically to NOLS, started with a chance encounter with a book. Books might be the best idea that anyone has ever had—most everybody who has had the privilege and good fortune to learn to read has had their life changed by the ideas in a book. For me, that book was *Voyaging on a Small Income* by Annie Hill. It's part how-to, part philosophy, and part memoir.

Annie and her husband, Pete, built a low-tech sailboat out of little more than plywood and gumption. They lived aboard this boat, *Badger*, for years. They were rarely in a marina, but instead sailed their boat in places such as the tropics, the Arctic, and across the Atlantic. The adventure of that type of life sounded pretty cool—but that's not what influenced me the most. I felt Annie's influence in my own life because they did so much, while seeming to need so little.

It was not mere thrift that drove them away from modern tools toward simplicity. The practice of using knowledge, determination, and simple tools is very empowering. I have found that the more I know, and the more practiced I become in basic technique, the fewer "things" I need in order to get by. That's true for many aspects of life, and it has influenced the way I prefer to travel in the backcountry. This is the big idea that Annie gave me, and it is eventually what led me to NOLS. NOLS backcountry living is stripped of extras, but it's not austere; it's comfortable living without schlepping around a house full of stuff.

I learned navigation theory from a collection of books, but the real practice of navigation happened alongside dozens of other NOLS instructors and many hundreds of NOLS students. We taught each other. Some of the most educational moments were hard won and very uncomfortable at the time. I appreciate the patience my students had with me as we sorted it all out. In the dark. In the rain. Thank you.

Thanks to Shannon Rochelle and Mark Tozer for their technical read and helpful comments, and to Helen Wilson for shepherding us all through the process of making a book. Thanks to the folks at NOLS who helped me to carve out chunks of time to make this book happen: Liz Tuohy, Alison Hudson, and Paul Cornia. Lastly, thanks to Kristi Herd for her inspiration and enthusiastic embrace of life as an adventure.

—Gene Trantham

Introduction

NOLS has been teaching wilderness navigation to novices and experts alike for more than 50 years. With hundreds of professional field instructors drawing on decades of collective experience, NOLS provides a complete and easy-to-follow navigation curriculum.

How to Use This Book

Students best learn to navigate when they acquire skills sequentially and, most importantly, experientially. *NOLS Wilderness Navigation* covers navigation essentials, using basic, reliable tools. It walks you through practical field exercises to help you become a competent and confident navigator, and uses a "light math" approach that minimizes common math errors. For readers who enjoy a mathematical challenge, a few optional nuggets are included. Use those nuggets only if you find them useful or entertaining; they are clearly marked, so you can skip over them if that's not your thing.

This book is built on the idea that you will read a chapter, practice the skills addressed, and move forward once you are ready. As with many outdoor skills, practice makes perfect.

If you are an experienced backcountry navigator, use this book as a reference or field guide to review topics of immediate interest. It is filled with tips to help you sharpen your skills with map, compass, altimeter, map software, and GPS.

This third edition of *NOLS Wilderness Navigation* differs from previous editions in a couple of important aspects:

1. We explicitly address different kinds of wilderness travelers. Most navigation books focus on land maps and backpacking/hiking, where extrapolating to other disciplines is fairly straightforward: Mountain bikers and skiers can use the same techniques using the same tools. For some activities, the conversion is less obvious, such as for sea kayakers, packrafters, stand-up paddleboarders, and small-boat sailors. Navigation topics apply to lots of different backcountry users, and we've tried to speak to some of them directly in this edition. Charts and maps are included, and we introduce terminology and tools that apply to both realms.

2. Digital tools are de-emphasized. This was done not because they are less important than they were when the second edition came out, but these days, digital tools evolve rapidly and new features are added almost more quickly than they can be reviewed. What you read here about digital tools may be wrong or out of date after next year's Consumer Electronics Show. More importantly, we are concerned that students learning to navigate from electronics will (a) engage more with their smartphone than with the environment through which they are traveling, and (b) become helpless and adrift when the cell coverage dies or the battery runs out. We want students to learn to navigate by learning principles and practicing with basic, robust, and reliable tools. Then we'll launch into electronic gadgetry to augment these critical skills.

Before Hitting the Trail

If you haven't spent much time in the wilderness, a little planning and preparation can save you a lot of grief—it may even save your life. As you gain experience, you will become comfortable hiking, canoeing, or skiing greater distances away from civilization. Before you get too far down that trail, consider some important steps:

1. Take a course in wilderness first aid. A good first-aid kit is not much use in the wilderness without adequate first-aid training.
2. Leave a detailed travel plan with a responsible adult before leaving on an expedition.
3. Pack essential gear. In addition to clothing and standard camping gear, there are several items you should not leave behind when you're heading away from roads and medical facilities:

   - Weatherproofed topo map(s)
   - Compass
   - Extra food
   - Extra clothing
   - First-aid kit
   - Lighter or weatherproof matches
   - Multi-tool or knife
   - Lined or weatherproof pack
   - Headlamp
   - Extra batteries
   - Identification
   - Medication or special medical equipment
   - Water bottle or hydration system
   - Means of water purification
   - Sunglasses and sunscreen (especially when you'll be in snowy environments)

It is worth making a practice of always carrying this gear with you into the backcountry. If this seems like a burden, consider that some of today's long-distance mountain runners train by running marathon distances with these items in their packs!

Leave No Trace

The Leave No Trace (LNT) Center for Outdoor Ethics (www .lnt.org) is an international organization devoted to promoting responsible outdoor recreation. In coordination with NOLS and various land management agencies, it has developed seven principles to guide backcountry visitors to minimize their impact on the outdoors. Keep them in mind so that you may help to preserve backcountry areas for future visitors.

1. Plan ahead and prepare.
2. Travel and camp on durable surfaces.
3. Dispose of waste properly.
4. Leave what you find.
5. Minimize campfire impact.
6. Respect wildlife.
7. Be considerate of other visitors.

Start with an online course from LNT, or jump straight into a live workshop or extensive training. This training will go into detail on each of these seven principles, and it will guide you toward specific techniques and how to apply them in various environments. "Dispose of waste properly," for example, is practiced differently on a wild and scenic river than it is on a glacier or in the desert.

A Few Final Words

As you build your navigation toolbox, beware of letting technology become a crutch. Keep the tool between your ears sharp, and ask yourself what you would do if you lost your GPS, your compass, or your map. As you learn to navigate on your own, you will be venturing into places where medical care can be far away and difficult to reach. Hopping from rock to rock across a creek that is 10 miles from the nearest road should be given more consideration than jumping over a flower bed in your front yard. Be conservative.

Until you are an expert at finding your way, you shouldn't venture into the wilderness alone. While it's not always possible, a group of at least four is best.

Finally, know and respect your group members' limitations. Have fun, but be safe!

CHAPTER 1 | TOOLS OF THE TRADE

The emphasis of this book is on simplicity of tools/equipment so as to better develop skills and practical experience. The more you know, the less you need. NOLS teaches navigation with fundamental tools, such as map and compass, because they are fail-safe. It is difficult to break a map so badly that it is worthless as a navigation tool. Compasses are easier to break than maps, but it still takes some work (and some bad luck). Compare them with more "hands-off" or automated tools such as GPS or smartphone apps. Electronics rely on batteries, a complex infrastructure, and a narrower range of acceptable use conditions, and they are much more fragile. The basic tools that are used to teach navigation concepts are the map and compass.

The standard tool for most backcountry land navigation is the US Geological Survey (USGS) topographic map, and other maps based on that standard. A few different maps will be displayed throughout this book, but the vast majority of map examples will employ the USGS map.

For coastal navigation, nautical charts are often used instead of maps. On occasion, these two terms may be used interchangeably in this text. While it is true that charts and maps are technically different types of documents, they can be used in much the same way. If you read "chart" and what you have is a "map," the techniques will still work.

Maps

A common type of map in the frontcountry is the planimetric map. Such maps contain no elevation data. They show everything in one plane, as if the world were flat. Planimetric maps are doubly distorted; they represent a spherical Earth as a flat plane (as most maps do), and they simplify the terrain to a flat plane rather than showing elevation/relief. A typical road map acquired at a gas station is an example of a planimetric map.

Some kinds of planimetric maps are suited for planning trips to wilderness, but most are not. Recreation and guidebook maps are good examples of a planimetric map with a specific and narrow focus suitable for backcountry travel. Recreation maps printed by government agencies, such as the Bureau of Land Management or the National Park Service, for a specific use, such as mountain biking or horsepacking, could be suitable. Guidebook maps are intended to get you to a specific trail or land feature. Some of these special-purpose maps feature trail profile charts telling you how long and steep a trail will be. You can use these maps, or a roadmap, to plan where you will

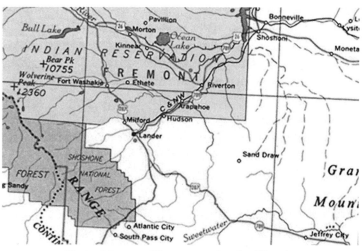

Planimetric map of the area near Lander, Wyoming

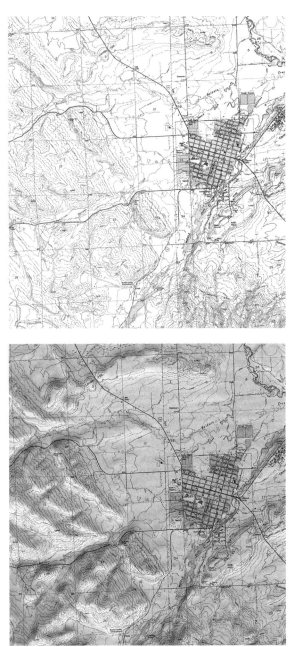

From top to bottom: more detailed topographic and topo relief maps of the area near Lander, Wyoming

enter the wilderness. For shorter trips on clearly marked trails, one of these may be all that you need.

For trips into the wilderness, however, planimetric maps are not adequate. For these trips you will need a topographic map. Topographic maps depict the shape of the land (its topography), in addition to many of the details found on planimetric maps (roads, buildings, rivers, etc.). The most common method for representing topography is through contour lines. The contour line system, which is explained in chapter 2, is a way to depict the convoluted shape of the terrain on a flat map.

SCALE

You may not be surprised to learn that there are different kinds of topo maps. The most important distinguishing feature of a topo is its scale. You can find topos in scales from 1:10,000 to 1:100,000 and up. Don't let the numbers scare you—they simply tell how much the map has been reduced. "1:24,000" is read as "one to twenty-four thousand." It is a ratio describing the relationship between distances measured on the map to distances measured in the real world. On a 1:24,000-scale map, for example, 1 inch on the map represents 24,000 inches (0.4 mile) on land, and 1 foot on the map equals 24,000 feet (4.5 miles) in the field.

A large-scale map has a smaller number in its ratio (e.g., 1:24,000 is a larger scale than 1:50,000). It represents a smaller area, but has more details. Large-scale maps are best for hiking, canoeing, or skiing. The smaller the map's scale, the larger the area it represents, and the more difficult it becomes to use it for wilderness travel. If you were hiking in the woods for several days, your location wouldn't change much on a map of the entire United States, for instance. Topo maps start to become difficult to use for land navigation when the scale gets below 1:100,000. The best scale for learning wilderness navigation is 1:24,000 or 1:25,000. In Alaska, you may be using a 1:63,360 map, where 1 inch equals 1 mile. In Europe and Canada, you will commonly find 1:50,000-scale maps, where 20 millimeters on the map equals 1 kilometer in the field.

In the United States, most backcountry travelers use US Geological Survey quadrangle maps, known as quads. USGS quads are developed from aerial photographs, which are used to determine where the contour lines should appear. US Topo maps refer to quadrangle topographic maps that are published in 2009 and later. The National Geographic Society, among others, produces a series of topo maps that feature shaded areas that provide a three-dimensional view. While these "relief" maps help in identifying topography, they are rarely found in large scales.

If you travel in the backcountry often enough, there will come a time when you will need to read your map in the rain. Weatherproofing maps can be as simple or as complicated as you wish to make it. One easy method of weatherproofing is to carry your maps in large plastic bags with zip tops. Ideally, they will be large enough to allow you to keep two to four folded maps together, for when you are traveling on the margins or corners of the maps. Disposable plastic bags are the lightest, and they are cheap and easy to replace when they get damaged. Use one bag for the map(s) you are currently using and another to store the rest of your maps in an accessible place.

IN THE MARGINS

Useful tools and pieces of information are located along the edges of topo maps. (The USGS calls this section of the map the "collar.") Expect the following elements on a USGS map:

- The name of the quadrangle appears in both the upper and lower corners on the right side of the map. The quad gets its name from a prominent land feature or population center located on the map. If you fold your map as shown in the illustration on page 7, you'll be able to read

the name from either side. This makes searching through
a pile of maps much easier.

- The date that the map was created or last revised is
located below the name in the bottom right corner.
While government agencies work to regularly update

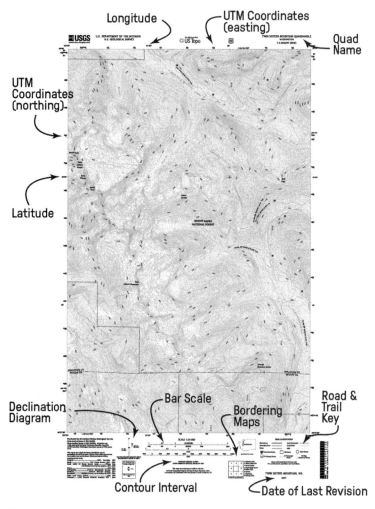

Parts of a standard USGS quad

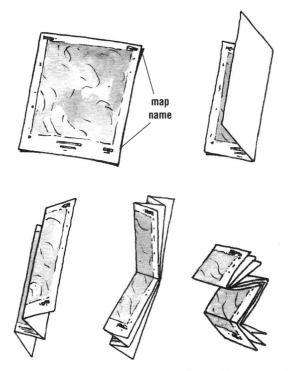

Fold your maps so that the map name can be read from either side.

quadrangles, they often cannot keep up with new roads or trails and other changes to the terrain. In some places, especially developing countries, a map made in the 1940s may be the most recent one that is available. Pay careful attention to the date on your map. The older the map, the more likely it is that glaciers have receded, ponds have dried up, trails and roads have moved, or landmarks have otherwise changed. That said, resist the urge to blame an out-of-date map if what you see does not line up with where you think you are, as it is quite possible that you have made a navigation error.

- The bar scale is located along the bottom center of the map. It consists of rulers that give distances in miles, feet, and kilometers.
- Below the scale is the contour interval. This is the elevation difference between contour lines. On 1:24,000-scale USGS quads, the contour interval is usually 40 feet (12.19 meters), although contour intervals of 20 and 80 feet are not uncommon. A contour interval of 50 feet (15.24 meters) or less will make it easier for you to learn to read contour lines. Contour intervals greater than 100 feet (30.48 meters) are rarely useful for foot travel outside of very large mountain ranges, like the Himalayas.
- The declination diagram is located on the lower left. It consists of two vectors that indicate the differences between magnetic north (MN), true north (TN), and grid north (GN). These distinctions are covered in chapter 4.
- The numbers running along the edges of the map are coordinates. These are useful in communicating your precise location over a radio or cellular phone (e.g., for a helicopter evacuation) or when you are using GPS. Often, maps have Universal Transverse Mercator (UTM) grid lines printed across the face of the map to assist in determining coordinates.
- Most quads also feature a key titled "Highways and Roads" or "Road Classification" in the bottom right. This key shows how roads and trails will be represented on the map.
- On older maps, the names of bordering maps appear in parentheses on every side and in the corners. Newer maps feature a diagram in the lower right showing the names of the adjoining quads.

MAP COLORS

USGS maps all use the same color system. Many other mapping authorities use the same standard. Look for examples of the following colors on the map you are using:

White indicates an area that is not forested. There may be snow, sand, boulders, tundra, sagebrush, or the occasional tree—anything other than dense forest or water. White doesn't automatically mean easy travel or great camping.

Green indicates vegetation. Solid green is a woodland forested area, defined by the USGS as having trees dense enough to conceal a platoon (around forty soldiers) in one acre. The border areas between green and white are often patchy and feature spotty tree coverage.

Blue means water. Solid blue shapes indicate lakes or ponds, while thick, continuous blue lines represent rivers. On older maps, dashed blue lines indicate seasonal streams, which run during the snowmelt in spring and early summer. Newer maps use thin, solid lines. White areas covered with tiny blue shrubs and dashes mark seasonal marshes in a clearing. Marshes that are underwater year-round appear on a blue background. Springs show up as tiny blue squiggles and are often labeled *spring*. Glaciers and permanent snowfields are enclosed by a dashed blue line. Blue is also used for contour lines on glaciers.

Black is used for names and human-made features—trails, dirt roads, boundaries, buildings, bridges, and mines. Black is also used for elevations that have been field-checked.

Red markings are reserved for US land survey lines, trail numbers, and major roads and boundaries. Many older US maps show numbered red grid lines that are part of a survey system called the US Public Land Survey System, which is often referred to as "township and range." Today, few but foresters and surveyors use this grid system. It can be helpful in measuring linear distance, since most of these grids are 1 square mile.

Purple is used for corrections or revisions that have been made to the original version of the map but have not been field-checked. Usually, the revisions will be dated on the bottom of the map.

Brown is reserved for contour lines and their elevations (except on glaciers).

Gray or pink areas indicate human developments and densely built-up areas such as towns or neighborhoods.

WHERE TO FIND US GOVERNMENT MAPS

store.usgs.gov—US Geological Survey Map Store
www.nps.gov—National Park Service
www.fs.fed.us—US Forest Service
www.blm.gov—Bureau of Land Management

Other mapping agencies have a web presence as well, and you should be able to locate the upstream source for printed maps with an internet search. Note that some countries consider topographic maps to be under the authority of that country's military. It may be the case that detailed maps are not available below a certain scale (if at all) because geospatial data can be considered a national security interest. For example, Chile's Instituto Geográfico Militar (www.igm.cl) publishes topographic maps for that country, but maps depicting critical disputed border areas with Argentina are not available for purchase by the general public.

Charts

Maps target land features, but they include information about water features. Charts have the opposite focus. They are detailed documents about the sea and its features, but also include land features that affect on-water navigation. Charts are occasionally useful for coastal navigation, even if just hiking along a beach.

Charts are the perfect choice for canoeists, sea kayakers, stand-up paddleboarders, and coastal hikers. They come in a wider range of "standard" scales than topographic maps, so they may be more detailed than a USGS topo for select areas of coastline.

The sea is a more complex environment to capture in a static paper chart than the (reasonably) unchanging land. The chart maker must consider tides, for example, which complicate the concept of shoreline. As the tides move the water level up and down, the border between ocean and land changes dramatically.

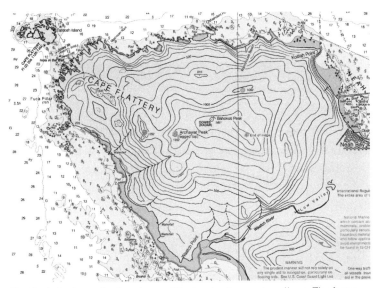

Nautical charts render the shape of the land using contour lines. The focus is on water features. This excerpt from chart 18485 Cape Flattery contains the locations of rocks, reefs, beaches, etc. The landforms are not represented with as much detail as on a topographic map.

COLORS

The color scheme for charts is dramatically different from that for topographic maps. The scheme below is from the National Oceanographic and Atmospheric Administration (NOAA), the chart maker for the United States. Similar schemes are in use for most other seafaring nations.

Brown is land. No effort is put toward distinguishing one type of land from another.

Green is intertidal. This zone is land when the tide is low, but water when the tide is high.

Blue is inland water or shallow ocean water.

White is ocean/water.

The decoding document for all chart features is *Chart No. 1*. This publication is available from the same source as your nautical chart. It explains in detail the use of color on nautical charts, as well as the symbols you may find on the chart.

Compass

A compass is a device that responds to the Earth's magnetic fields. It points toward magnetic north (which is near but not in exactly the same place as the North Pole; this will be explained in detail later). All the plastic, rulers, numbers, and arrows are there to make a compass easier to use, but its essence is its north-pointing magnet. When used properly, it can help to determine cardinal directions from almost any location on the planet.

FEATURES OF A COMPASS

This illustration shows a compass with numerous features. At the very least, your compass must have a needle, bezel, and base plate. If you plan to travel in the backcountry regularly, or if you need a high level of precision (to compete in orienteering,

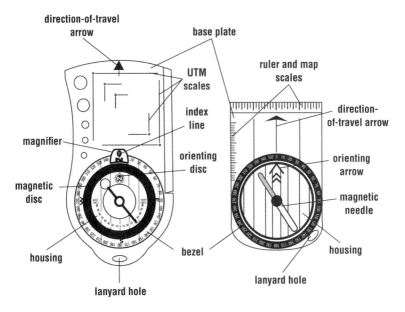

Parts of basic disc and needle compasses

for example), it is worth investing in a more advanced compass. If you already own a compass, pull it out now and see if you can identify the following parts:

Needle
The needle, which is made of magnetized iron, balances on a pivot so that it can swing easily in any direction. The north-seeking end of traditional compass needles is red. Some have a convenient glow-in-the-dark stripe. Some compasses use an all-black needle with a hollow circle on the north-seeking end for improved accuracy.

Housing and Bezel
The housing is the plastic liquid-filled vial that surrounds the needle. The needle is in a nonfreezing damping liquid so that it doesn't move erratically or freeze in subzero temperatures. The

bezel (also called an azimuth ring) is the rotating dial around the housing. It is marked with 360 degrees, usually in 2-degree increments. As you turn the bezel, you turn the entire housing. On the bottom of the housing on most compasses are meridian lines and an orienting arrow. The meridian lines can help you determine declination. On most compasses, the orienting arrow looks like a tiny shed that outlines the needle. The orienting shape on the base plate is used to outline, or "box," the magnetic needle when determining your bearing or direction of travel.

Base Plate

The base plate is the rectangular piece of plastic on which the housing is mounted. It is often transparent and marked with rulers or UTM grid readers. It is also marked with a direction-of-travel arrow that, along with the orienting arrow on the bottom of the housing, helps you take and follow bearings. The index line is where bearings are read.

Sighting Mirror

A sighting mirror is a small mirror that folds over the top of the housing to close the compass. Compasses with a sighting mirror are sometimes called prismatic compasses. The mirror is used to align the compass with distant objects when taking or following a bearing. The advantage of the mirror is that it allows you to adjust the azimuth while sighting a distant object. Tilting the mirror toward you enables you to view the reflection of the orienting arrow while holding the compass at eye level and an arm's length away. This adds a significantly higher level of accuracy when using bearings. While most sighting mirrors cover the entire base plate when closed, some newer compasses use a lower-profile mirror to allow a better view of your objective and more accurate sighting.

FEATURES OF ADVANCED COMPASSES

Lanyard

This is a fancy name for the cord attached to the base plate. Many lanyards have a sliding plastic toggle of some sort that can be used to measure distance on a map. While most folks use the toggle and lanyard to wear the compass around their neck when it's not in use, beware that the lanyard can occasionally catch on thick brush or climbing gear.

Declination Adjustment

Many compasses feature an adjustable orienting arrow. This allows you to set the declination on your compass so that you do not have to add or subtract in the field while switching between magnetic and true bearings—a welcome convenience after an exhausting day in the mountains. Some compasses with a declination adjustment have a tiny screwdriver attached to the lanyard for turning the declination screw on the back of the bezel. Others may be adjusted without a screwdriver by pinching and rotating the housing while holding the azimuth ring still.

Global Pivot

Ignore this advanced feature unless you are planning to use your compass outside North America. A global pivot allows the needle to tilt vertically in such a way that it is not affected by the Earth's different magnetic dip zones.

Clinometer

Some compasses have a second free-moving needle attached to the pivot inside the bezel. This nonmagnetic arrow is usually black and is used to measure the angle of a slope in the field when the compass is tilted on its side. This is a critical tool for those needing to assess avalanche potential.

Magnifying Glass

Even if your vision is good, it is occasionally nice to have a small magnifying glass built into the base plate for reading tiny names and map features.

TYPES OF COMPASSES

Special compasses are used in a wide variety of outdoor endeavors. There are specialized compasses for sea kayaking, sailing, adventure racing, and caving, just to name a few. New digital compasses are appearing on the market every day. While many compasses will perform some of the functions you need for backcountry travel, only base plate compasses can meet all of your navigational needs.

There are many different base plate compasses from which to choose. Simple models are less expensive but lack sighting mirrors, declination adjustments, and other special features. While they are adequate for land navigation in most areas, they require you to do a little more work or mental arithmetic if you are traveling exclusively on bearings. There are also compasses that feature a mirror but no declination adjustment, or vice versa.

Advanced or full-featured compasses are the best for wilderness navigation. If you are new to backcountry travel, paying for mirrors, lanyards, and clinometers might seem like a waste. If you have yet to purchase a full-featured compass, read the rest of this chapter, and then decide whether the extra expense is worth it.

A number of watches and smartphones feature digital compasses. While digital compasses are becoming more accurate, they should still be viewed as a backup tool, and not a replacement for old-fashioned analog base plate compasses. Watches are more difficult to accurately sight with and are almost useless for taking bearings from a map. This is not to say that they don't have a place in the backcountry, however—many of them also feature very accurate altimeter-barometers, which will be discussed more in chapter 6.

If you intend to use a digital compass to navigate, or if there is a chance that you might use it, be sure that it is calibrated properly and that the declination is set correctly. Most digital compasses are easier to calibrate at home than in the field. If you're not sure if yours is calibrated correctly, compare it to an analog compass.

Digital watch compass

POTENTIAL COMPASS PROBLEMS

For those traveling to high elevations or cold climates, it is common for a vacuum bubble to form within the compass housing. This occurs because the damping fluid contracts faster than the tightly sealed housing. The bubble should not affect the compass's performance and should disappear when you return to warmer temperatures. If the bubble does not disappear after a day or two, however, you could have a leak in the housing seal and a broken compass.

On the other end of the temperature spectrum, extreme heat can ruin a compass quickly. If the plastic itself doesn't melt, the liquid may overexpand and break the housing. When in hot environments, try not to leave the compass in direct sunlight for long periods of time.

Just as they can ruin watches and other plastic navigational tools, chemicals can also ruin your compass. DEET, found in many insect repellents, is a common culprit in dissolving the ink off your compass and possibly eating through the housing. Be careful when handling any potentially harmful substances.

GPS

We'll get into more detail with GPS in its own chapter. We're focusing on basic tools and skill development, so set down that GPS and learn about navigational concepts first.

CHAPTER 2 | TERRAIN ASSOCIATION

In this era of modern navigation devices, it is still true that the single most important skill for a navigator to have is the ability to read a map. Map-reading abilities (and having the right map) has made or broken countless trips to wild places. Regardless of your reasons for venturing into the wild, little else matters when you are lost. On expeditions, navigators are often seen as heroes or fools, depending mainly on their ability to match their location to a point on the map.

The step-by-step skill progression in this chapter will help you to successfully navigate using the most fundamental tools. As you work through this chapter—and during your first few times in the field—leave the compass in your pocket. Start the learning process by studying the shape of the land itself. While some outdoor educators introduce map and compass together, NOLS instructors have found that students can navigate in many areas without using a compass. In any case, students develop map-reading skills faster without one. Extra tools, even essential ones like the compass, can distract focus from the surroundings. The first step in becoming a navigator is learning to pay attention to the terrain.

As you begin to recognize distant land features by sight, start to compare them with what you see on the map. Only after you are comfortable associating terrain with the images on the map should you begin to use your compass. More advanced gadgetry, such as altimeters and GPS receivers, should not be added to your toolbox until after you have mastered the basics of map and compass. If you learn to read maps well, you may be able to achieve your backcountry goals without relying on electronics.

Reading a Map or Chart

Map-reading skills are much like any other learned skill—they grow through practice. Practice when consequences are mild and the degree of difficulty is low. Do not wait to practice until you are lost, deep in the mountains, alone, at night, and during a blizzard.

Start with the basics of your map's symbology—the signs and symbols used to represent features. This basic knowledge can be developed in the comfort of your living room.

Open a topo map and lay it out in front of you so that you can see its entire surface. The top margin of the map always represents north; the other cardinal directions follow.

Basic Directions

You probably know that the four main cardinal directions are north, south, east, and west. As you can see on the compass rose below, they can be divided into northwest (NW), northeast (NE), southwest (SW), and southeast (SE). Those directions can be further broken down into north-northeast (NNE), east-northeast (ENE), east-southeast (ESE), south-southeast (SSE), south-southwest (SSW), west-southwest (WSW), west-northwest (WNW), and north-northwest (NNW).

SYMBOLOGY

Terrain association is two related skills. They are:

- Forming a picture in your head of the real-world terrain, based on the information on the map or chart.
- Forming a picture in your head of what the map should look like, based on what you see in the terrain around you.

To do this, you need to know how features in the real world are represented on a map. This is the symbology employed on a map or chart. Hundreds of symbols are used on standardized topographic maps to represent common objects, and still more symbols are used on nautical charts. Even so, you can do a surprisingly good job of terrain association by knowing just a few of the most crucial symbols. Because terrestrial maps and nautical charts use different symbology schemes, we'll cover them separately. Many concepts will cross over between maps and charts (contour lines, for example), but they may be represented differently.

US Topo Standard Symbols

Most mapping authorities use a very similar, if not identical, standard to that of the US Topo for symbols and colors. Some important symbology from the US Topo standard:

PERENNIAL STREAM	
INTERMITTENT STREAM	
PERENNIAL LAKE	
INTERMITTENT LAKE	
ROCK	

RAILROAD	──┼─┼─┼─┼─┼─┼─┼─┼─┼─┼──
EXPRESSWAY	━━━━━━━━━━━━━
SECONDARY HWY	▬▬▬▬▬▬▬▬▬
LOCAL ROAD	─────────────
AWD	─ ─ ─ ─ ─ ─ ─ ─ ─ ─
TRAIL	- - - - - - - - - - - - - - -

INDEX	⌒ 8000 ⌒
INTERMEDIATE	⌒⌒
DEPRESSION INDEX	⌒ 4000 ⌒
DEPRESSION INTERMEDIATE	⌒ 4000 ⌒

Chart Standard Symbols

Chart symbols are collected in a special catalog called *Chart No. 1*. Marine navigation, broadly speaking, encompasses the idea of crossing oceans; it is an international undertaking. For this reason, most jurisdictions agree on chart symbology, and most modern charts resemble one another.

The US version of *Chart No. 1* is published by NOAA and is available for download. It is also available in print form at a nominal cost. Some important examples:

LIGHTHOUSES – PAGE 76 FROM CHART-1

The example from Line-1, INT column. Text is "Major light, minor light, light, lighthouse"

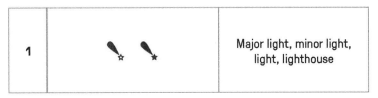

CONTOUR LINES – PAGE 18 FROM CHART-1

Graphic from Line-13, INT column. Text is "Contour lines with values and spot height"

MEASURING DISTANCE

You can measure any distance on a map or chart using a string. Non-elastic strings work best. A shoelace, a piece of "parachute" cord, or the lanyard on your compass will work fine. You may be tempted to use a straightedge for measuring distances, and it'll work like a champ if the distance you need to measure is straight "as the crow flies." It is much more likely that you want to know the distance along a route, such as a trail, coastline, or river. The string method is easier and more accurate in these real-world situations.

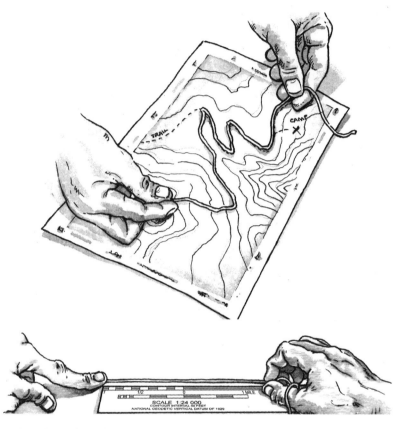

By using a piece of string, you can determine the mileage for even the most winding trails.

To measure the distance between two points:

1. Place your map on a flat surface.
2. Keeping one end of your string on the start point, place the string along your planned route so that it follows it exactly.

3. Pinch the spot in the string where it intersects your destination.

4. Keeping that spot pinched between your fingers, stretch the string out along the scale at the bottom of the map. This will provide you with your linear distance. You may have to move the string across the scale several times. Keep in mind that 1:24,000-scale quads have a scale that represents 2 miles in total length, but with a 0 in the middle and 1s on either end.

Nautical charts often do not have a distance scale on them, mostly due to tradition. Mariners measure distances in nautical miles. A nautical mile is defined as a minute of latitude, which works out to about 1.85 kilometers or 1.15 statute miles. To measure distance on a nautical chart, use the same string exercise as for a map, tracing the string along the feature or route that you want to measure. Rather than comparing this against a distance scale, hold the string up against the latitude markings on the left or right border of the chart. The number of minutes of latitude equals the number of nautical miles.

Modern charts may also feature a distance scale. If that feature exists, you can use it in the same way that you would on a map.

READING CONTOUR LINES

The most important skill in terrain association is the ability to visualize landforms. The shape of the land is represented on topos and charts using contour lines. Reading and understanding contour lines is the essence of map reading. While at first they may seem like a jumbled mess, once you understand them, they will tell you volumes about the terrain through which you are traveling.

Contour lines are imaginary lines that trace a path of equal elevation. If you were to follow the path of one such line on land, you would be walking at a constant elevation, neither

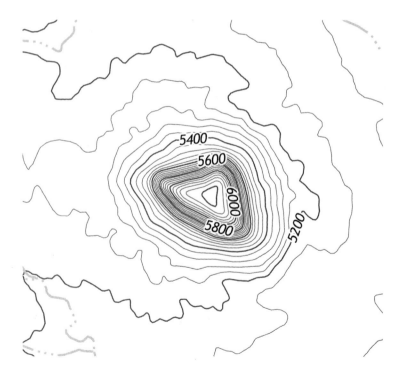

climbing nor descending. The quintessential natural contour line is the shoreline of a lake.

The elevation difference between each line remains the same throughout a given map. This means that you can easily tell how steep an area is by how close together the contour lines are spaced. Where the lines are spread far apart, the land is fairly flat. Where the lines are close together, it is steep. In a very flat area, such as that found in some deserts, there may be only a few contour lines on the entire map. In a very steep, cliff-filled area, many contour lines crowd together.

The feature in the topographical map shown is Merrick Butte, located within the Monument Valley Navajo Tribal Park in Arizona. Note the concentric contour lines, which indicate a gain in elevation. Outside of the 5,200-foot contour line, the lines are spread apart, indicating fairly flat terrain. Between 5,200 and 5,600 feet, the lines are spaced regularly and much closer together. Regularly spaced lines indicate consistent slope.

A view from the north of Mount Saint Helens in Washington. Note the open crescent shape of the ridge encircling the cone.

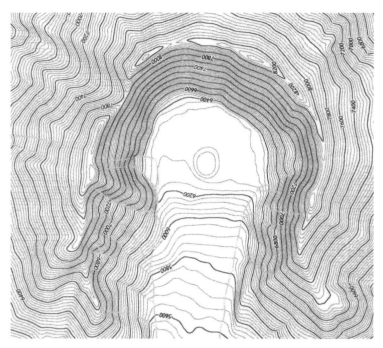

The US Topo contour lines that represent Mount Saint Helens. The map has been inverted (south at the top, north at the bottom) to better match the previous photo. Note how steep the terrain is on the inside of the crescent ridge. Also notice that the small mound in the middle of the crater is shown. The smoke is not.

Note that between 5,600 and 6,000 feet, the lines are spaced closer still. This indicates steeper terrain. When the lines are indistinguishable from one another, the terrain is essentially vertical. Above 6,000 feet, the lines space out again, indicating that the top of this feature is relatively flat.

The contour lines in the Mount Saint Helens topographical map tell a complex story. Note the obvious crescent-shaped ridge that opens on one side. The contour lines are regularly spaced outside of this crescent, and the elevation increases as you approach the ridge. "Inside" the crescent, the contour lines

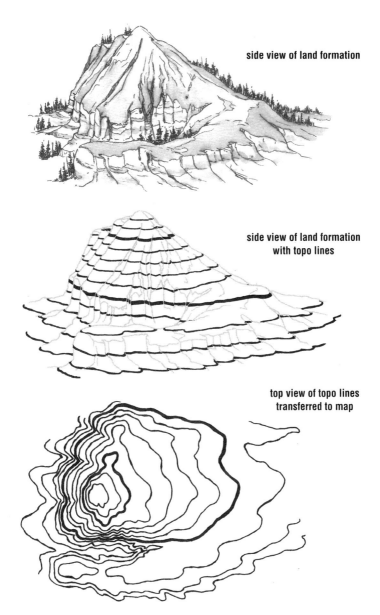

side view of land formation

side view of land formation
with topo lines

top view of topo lines
transferred to map

Contour lines allow a two-dimensional map to represent elevation changes.
Notice the familiar shape of this particular land formation. You can achieve
a similar effect by making a fist and drawing concentric circles around your
knuckles—the view from above is like looking at a topo map.

are closer together (steeper terrain), and the elevation decreases as you move toward the center of the crescent. Notice that in the center of the crescent, the terrain is fairly flat (contour lines spaced wide apart), with a small dome right in the middle of this flat space.

Index contours are the heavier lines that include elevation numbers. On 1:24,000-scale US topos (with contour intervals of 40 feet), index lines are 200 feet apart in elevation. Between each pair of index contours are four light-brown lines that do not have marked elevations. These are known as intermediate contours, and they are usually 40 feet apart. The distance between any two successive contours is known as the contour interval.

Converging contours are contour lines that appear as one thick brown line. When contours converge, they indicate a cliff—vertical or near-vertical terrain. Unless you're going rock or ice climbing, avoid converging contour lines.

Supplementary contours only appear in relatively flat terrain. These are dotted contour lines that mark the interval halfway between two intermediate lines.

Contour lines show both landforms and slope gradient. Tightly spaced lines indicate a rapid change in elevation; loosely spaced lines indicate flatter terrain. Examine the contour lines in the Merrick Butte example to see how slope is represented by how closely spaced the contour lines are.

HANDS-ON ACTIVITY: MODELING CONTOUR LINES
The following activity has helped NOLS students develop a sense for topography: Build models of landforms using sand and a simplified set of contour lines found on a map or chart. The model of the landform should be to scale.

This exercise can also be done in reverse: Examine a landform (of any size) and practice drawing the contour lines that might be used to map it.

As you get better at reading contour lines, increase the challenge of your practice. Just before you travel around a corner, use your map to predict what the land will look like in the new view. Try to "see" the terrain before you arrive.

TERRAIN ASSOCIATION FOR LAND TRAVELERS

The ability to recognize land features and to match them to details on the printed map (and vice versa) is called terrain association. Most of the time, you will be associating terrain with the contours depicted on the map, but other features can be helpful as well: locations of trails, roads, rivers, lakes, conspicuous buildings, etc. Terrain association is crucial to navigating with a topographic map. Good navigators are able to look at a map and see the entire route in their mind's eye. The best navigators can describe what a hiking day may look like to the rest of the folks in their party just by looking at the map. An example of how this can help in day-to-day planning can be seen here:

We shouldn't overdress starting out because we'll be heading up a steep hill in the morning sun. As the terrain levels out, we'll reach a plateau with a beautiful view of Angel Peak. We might want to take our first break there, and snap some photos. We should also refill our water bottles at the stream there before we head across the dry plateau. We'll be descending into a shady, tree-filled valley to the north by noon. There may be patches of snow. We'll drop down some steep switchbacks for an hour or so before popping out into a clearing on the valley floor, where we'll cross a small river. We should make sure that the gear in our packs is waterproofed. There should be great camping in the meadow after we cross the creek. If we leave now, taking breaks and traveling at the pace we traveled yesterday, we should be in camp by 3 or 3:30 p.m.

You should think of the land you are traveling on in terms of hills, drainages, and ridges. Being able to identify these three basic features by looking at the contour lines on a map will go a long way toward successful navigation. If you have a topo map handy, try to identify examples of each on your map.

Once you develop an eye for land features, you will be able to look at a route and easily determine whether it ascends or descends the features it crosses. Until then, read the elevations on the index lines to determine if the numbers are going up or down.

Summit/Peak

A summit, or peak, is the highest point on any hill or mountain. A small circle surrounded by increasingly larger shapes usually indicates a summit—as the circles grow larger, the elevation drops. Significant summits with verified elevations are often indicated on maps by a surveyor's benchmark (marked *BM*), a triangle, an X, or elevation.

Ridge/Spur

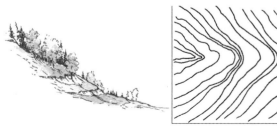

A ridge, or spur, is a relatively narrow area of elevation descending from a summit. It is the topographic opposite of a drainage or valley. A ridge is indicated in contour lines by rough U or V shapes, with the curve of the U pointing downhill.

Drainage

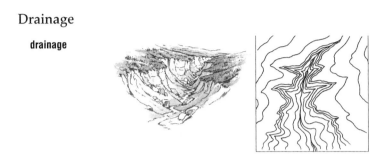

drainage

A drainage is a collecting area that water will flow to. There are countless names for the different kinds of drainages, depending on their size and location. Gullies, couloirs, valleys, arroyos, crevasses, and canyons are all drainages. Drainages are indicated in contour lines by V shapes, where the apex of the V points uphill.

While mountains do have a general cone shape, their sides are textured by ridges and drainages. If you look at a large aerial photograph of virtually any mountain, you will probably see instances of both descending from the summit. They tend to alternate—ridge, drainage, ridge, drainage, and so on.

Saddle

saddle

A saddle is a low point on a ridge between two summits. The contour lines of a saddle form an hourglass shape. Saddles are usually the easiest route from one side of a chain of hills to the other. There are many different kinds of saddles. A saddle between two glaciers is called a col. Very steep and rocky saddles are sometimes called notches. Saddles large enough to drive a car through are called passes.

Depression

depression

A depression is a low point on the terrain. Depressions are notable for being isolated sudden drops, rather than a gradual or fluid reduction in elevation (such as a river drainage). A sinkhole is an example of a depression.

TERRAIN ASSOCIATION FOR COASTAL TRAVELERS

Contour lines and topography are important for water navigation as well. Reading the shape of islands, for example, can be helpful in distinguishing one island from another. The contour interval on nautical charts is typically much greater than that on topographic maps, so the topo will be more helpful for reading the shape of the land.

Charts label the maximum height of islands, so they can be distinguished from one another. Units (feet, meters) aren't important, as you can see in the example below that one island is 50 percent taller than the other. As you look at an island group, you can orient yourself with just this information: The islands are roughly N-S, with the taller island to the south.

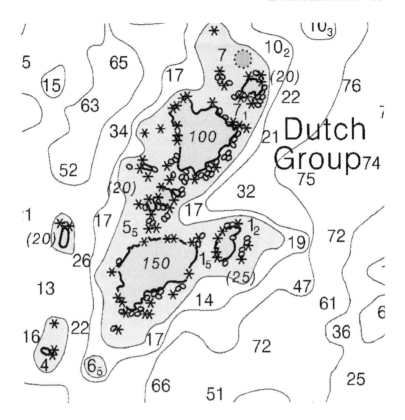

ESTIMATING STEEPNESS

The measurement of a hill's steepness is called its slope angle. If you are traveling in the mountains, you may need to determine slope angle to decide whether or not to follow a particular route. An angle from 0 to 5 degrees is fairly easy; you may not even notice that it is slightly inclined. From 5 to 25 degrees, you will certainly know that you're going uphill. Slopes above 15 degrees will take more time to travel upon than flat terrain, which you should factor into your route planning. A moderate slope (25 to 35 degrees) can be a significant challenge, particularly if you are traveling off-trail with a backpack. Because of the risks associated with travel on steep slopes (45+ degrees), these should be reserved for those with mountaineering training. A 90-degree slope is a vertical wall or cliff.

On slopes over 35 degrees, you should start to be concerned with falling rocks. The safest way to deal with steep, rocky slopes is to avoid them. If you must ascend one, keep your group close together, and follow a zigzag pattern on the way up to minimize the chance of someone knocking rocks down onto those below. Before even thinking about climbing a snowy slope of more than 25 degrees, seek out a trained professional to learn how to use an ice ax and assess avalanche danger. If in doubt, avoid steep terrain all together.

As you travel in mountainous terrain with your map, you will develop an eye for how steep a hill is by looking at contour lines. The closer the contours are to each other, the steeper the hill. There are several ways to get a more precise idea of how steep a slope may be. The easiest is by using a slope gauge. This navigational tool is designed for a given scale (e.g., 1:24,000) and provides the slope angle for a series of contour lines. It can help you develop an eye for terrain association. You can find one at an outdoor retailer or online.

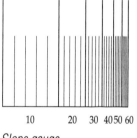

Slope gauge

To determine the slope angle using a slope gauge:

1. Make sure the scale of the gauge matches the scale of the map.
2. Draw a straight line along the route you plan to take up the hill.
3. Move the gauge along the line until a section of the gauge aligns with the contours at the steepest part of your route. The index lines should overlap precisely.
4. The number indicated on the gauge is the slope angle for that part of the hill.

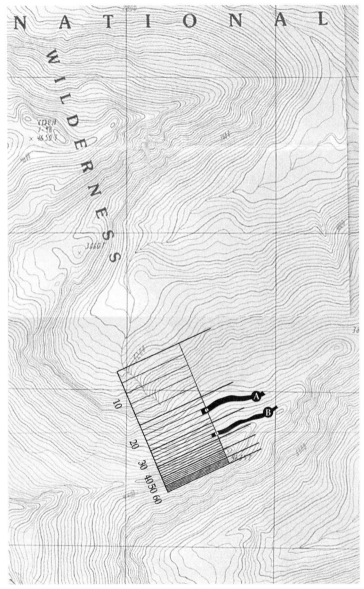

A slope gauge allows you to measure the slope angle at a given point on a topo map. The point along contour "A" has a slope angle of 20 degrees; the point along contour "B" has an angle of 30 degrees.

If you are a math geek, or just prefer to have more factors to consider when planning routes, you may be interested in the grade of the slope. If you've driven in the mountains, you've probably seen road signs warning of a steep grade. The grade is the change in height of a slope divided by its distance (as the crow flies, not the distance on the ground), rendered as a percentage. For example, for a slope that covers a distance of 400 feet and drops 100 feet, the grade is 25 percent. A slope 400 feet long and 400 feet high has a grade of 100 percent (45 degrees). As a general rule, you should avoid slopes where the height is equal to or greater than the distance, unless you are mountaineering.

TOTAL ELEVATION GAIN

Measuring the elevation you will gain on a particular route before starting out allows you to estimate how much time and energy you will expend. Measuring elevation is as simple as counting contour lines. Be careful, however, not to count the lines in which you are losing elevation. It may help to double-check your calculations by looking at the elevation of each contour line. Are the numbers increasing or decreasing as you travel along your route?

At first glance, it may be tempting to add or subtract the elevation change between your origin and your final destination. However, this will not give you an accurate idea of what your travel time may be. You will encounter many ups and downs during your hiking day that will slow you down. For example, if you start on the North Rim of the Grand Canyon and want to travel to the South Rim (ending the day at nearly the same elevation), you cannot neglect the almost one mile of elevation that you will have to regain as you climb back out of the canyon. If you ignored the elevation gain, your travel time would be off by at least six hours—try explaining that mistake to your exhausted hiking partners as you crawl into camp in the dark! A hike such as this might need to be broken into two or three days.

The following guidelines are estimates based on typical speeds for an average party:

- 1,000 feet of elevation gain = time and effort of 1 additional mile; 200 meters of elevation gain = time and effort of 1 additional kilometer
- 2 miles (about 3 kilometers) on flat trail with full expedition backpacks takes approximately 1 hour
- 1 mile (about 1.5 kilometers) of off-trail travel with a full expedition pack takes approximately 1 hour

ORIENTING YOUR MAP WITHOUT A COMPASS

To orient your map, you must turn it so that the cardinal directions match those on land. An oriented map helps you determine your exact location and what lies between you and your destination. There are two ways to do this without a compass—by using terrain association or by using the sun and the stars. Practice both methods, and learn to use them together whenever possible.

Using Terrain Association to Orient Your Map

The first step in terrain association is to locate a nearby terrain feature that is easy to find on your map. Features such as trails, ridges, and drainages are a good starting point. If you can't find a land feature that you can positively match to your map, you won't be able to orient your map with terrain association alone. Next, rotate your map until the shape on the map is aligned with the terrain feature that you can see.

The very best time to orient your map using terrain association is when you know with certainty where you are. Orient your map or chart at the trailhead, before you set out. Identify macro features on the map, associating them with the terrain that you see around you; for example, "Here we are at the

Beaver Lodge trailhead. That peak to the northwest is Alison Cone. The trail runs roughly south from here." Then verify that the map is oriented correctly. Take a look around to make sure that the positions of what you see on land match those that you see on the map, and that the cardinal directions correspond to shadows cast by the sun.

Using the Sun and Stars to Orient Your Map

You probably learned in grade school that the sun rises in the east and sets in the west. This is in essence true, although a rising sun is almost never due east. How far north or south of east the sun rises depends on the time of sunrise, which in turn depends on latitude. In the northern hemisphere, the sun is always directly east at solar 6 a.m. (this is true whether it is above or below the horizon), directly south at solar noon, and directly west at solar 6 p.m. This means that you can orient your map precisely if you know the solar time at your location. In

In the northern hemisphere at midday, the shadows of vertical objects will point north.

most places in the US, solar time is the same as the time on your watch during standard time (winter), and it's one hour behind the time on your watch during daylight saving time. Alaska, Hawaii, and places that don't follow standard conventions of daylight saving time require a bit more time conversion effort.

In the middle of the day, in many locations, you can use the shadows of vertical objects to determine north. In the northern hemisphere, the sun does not cross directly overhead as it does at the equator. It passes just to the south. This is the reason why there is more shade and snow on the north faces of North American mountains. The shadow of a perfectly straight tree points north at solar noon. The length of this shadow varies, depending on latitude. The farther north of the equator, the longer the shadow. At the equator, there is no shadow at all, and in the southern hemisphere, the shadow points south.

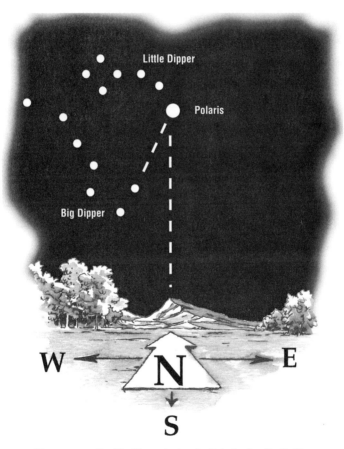

You can use the Big Dipper to locate Polaris, the North Star.

You can also find north using the stars. In the northern hemisphere, this can be as simple as finding Polaris, often referred to as the North Star. Polaris is most easily located by relating it to the Big Dipper—an easily spotted asterism in most northern latitudes. Look for the two stars at the end of this familiar constellation, the ones that lie farthest from the handle. They form a straight line that points directly toward Polaris, which is known as the North Star because it always lies directly

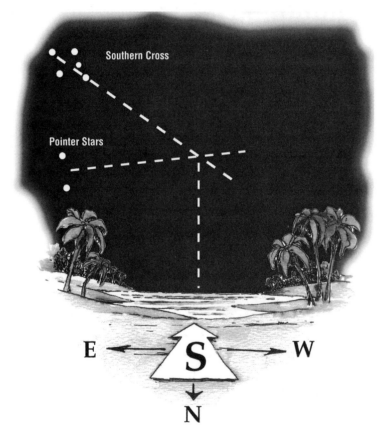

In the southern hemisphere, navigators can use the Southern Cross for guidance.

to the north. On a clear night in the northern hemisphere, Polaris is a bright star that stands alone, and as the night progresses, the other stars appear to revolve around it. The farther north you are, the higher it is positioned in the sky and the more difficult it will be to tell which direction is north. If you are in a southern location, the Big Dipper may be below the horizon, offering no help in locating Polaris.

In places such as southern Chile or New Zealand, the Southern Cross is often used for direction. This constellation is less than half the size of the Big Dipper. It lacks a bright star in the middle, so it actually resembles a kite more than it does a cross. If you draw an imaginary line along the long beam of the cross and another one from the two "pointer stars" near the cross, the intersection marks true south.

Exercises

Exercise 1: Writing a Travel Plan

A travel plan is an itinerary that provides an overview of your intended route. There are at least three good reasons to write a travel plan:

1. The process of writing a travel plan forces you to practice critical map-reading skills.
2. A well-written travel plan can serve as a tool to monitor your route progress and stay on track while you are in the field.
3. A travel plan can help someone find you in case of an emergency.

Unlike many of the exercises in this book, you can (and should) write a travel plan before going into the field. Make sure your plan includes the following:

1. The name of each person in your party and what equipment they are carrying. Identify important roles such as expedition leader, navigator, climbing leader, and so on.

2. Your planned origin and destination for each day of your trip. Be as precise and descriptive as you can. If your destination is not next to an obvious land feature, include directions and distances to three recognizable features. Ask yourself if you would be able to find your location if someone handed you this description.

3. A detailed route description using named map features and cardinal directions.

4. Time/distance calculations.
   a. The linear distance from your origin to your destination.
   b. The perceived distance between origin and destination; add 1 mile per 1,000 feet of elevation gain.
   c. The moving travel time in hours, as determined by dividing the perceived distance (in miles or kilometers) by your party's average rate of travel (in miles or kilometers per hour).
   d. The total travel time. This includes moving travel, plus time for breaks, river crossings, and any other expected delays.
   e. The estimated time of arrival (ETA): your estimated time of departure (ETD) plus your total travel time.

5. Contingency plans and information. These include alternate campsites and rendezvous points, anticipated hazards and obstacles, and potential causes for delay. This information should be more detailed in situations where there are additional hazards or unknowns that might prevent you from reaching your destination.

Sample Travel Plan
Lake Lunker Fly-Fishing Expedition—Day Two (8/9/2018)

1. **Team Members:** Missy White (expedition leader)—cookware and stove; Scott Kane—rain fly and tent poles; Stacy Wells—tent body, bear spray, and GPS; Dave Glenn—maps, compass, and first-aid kit.

2. **Point of Origin:** ½ mile south of Lake Watonga, ⅔ mile northeast of the summit of Mount Kalamazoo, and 1½ miles southwest of the Snake River at 10,200 feet.
   Destination: The north shore of Lake Lunker between Trail 456 and Big Lunker Creek.

3. **Route Description:**
   Leg 1: Leave camp hiking SE on the Highline Trail. Climb the switchbacks to the intersection of Highline and Trail 456, gaining 900 feet of elevation.
   Leg 2: Hike south on Trail 456 for 4½ miles, passing on the east side of Mount Kalamazoo, handrailing Big Lunker Creek, and descending 350 feet to the intersection of Big Lunker and Small Lunker creeks.
   Leg 3: Cross SL Creek, and head SSW off-trail, gaining 100 feet for ¼ mile up a forested slope to the destination, 10,950 feet.

4. **Time/Distance Calculations:**
   a. 6½ miles of linear distance
   b. 6½ miles + 1 mile (1,000 feet of elevation gain) = 7½ miles perceived distance
   c. 7½ miles ÷ 2 miles per hour = 3¾ hours of travel time
   d. 3¾ hours + 1 hour (lunch, water breaks, and creek crossing) = 4¾ hours total time
   e. 9:30 a.m. departure time + 4¾ hours = 2:15 p.m. ETA

5. **Contingency Plans:** If Small Lunker Creek is too fast or too big to cross, we will camp in the small meadow ¼

mile north of the intersection of Big and Small Lunker creeks.

Write travel plans for your next few trips into the backcountry, or for an imaginary trip based on your USGS quads. Spend a day navigating entirely using your travel plan rather than reading your map. Are you able to find your way following the directions you've written?

Exercise 2: Practicing Terrain Association

The most important navigation skill to develop is your ability to recognize land features and associate them with the contour lines that you see on your map. This exercise will help you develop your eye for land features, without even breaking a sweat.

First, find an area to visit with a good view. Choose a location you are familiar with and that is high and clear of anything that would block your view—a hilltop, a high roadside pullout, a ridge, or even a rooftop in a hilly, rural area. For learning purposes, it's best to find a place where there are big, recognizable land features—such as mountains, hills, valleys, or small drainages—that will be visible from one spot. The farther you can see, the better.

Make sure you have topo maps that will cover all of the areas you can see from your vantage point. In places that fall near map edges or corners, you may need up to four maps. For this exercise, you will also need some blank paper, pencils, a writing surface, and about 45 minutes. A camp chair, binoculars, and colored pencils are also nice, if you have them.

Once you are in the right spot with the right materials, orient the map. Place rocks on the corners to keep the map from blowing away. Find your location and mark it. Then spend 10 to 15 minutes studying the map and identifying as many corresponding land features as you can.

Next, put the real map away and try to sketch your own topo map based on the land features you see. Start your hand-drawn map by drawing any visible drainages and roads. Without peeking at the map, try to draw them to the same scale as your printed map by looking at the land. Then, mark the locations of all of the summits you can see.

You are now ready to add contour lines. If you are in a mountainous area, try to draw in just the index contours (every 200 feet on a 1:24,000-scale map). Take your time, and try to be as accurate as possible. Start from summits, and draw the consecutive contours that descend from them. Try to represent all of the visible ridges, drainages, and bodies of water. Use binoculars if you have them.

Once you have finished your sketch, compare your map(s) to your drawing. Obviously, the level of detail and precision will not be the same, but try to determine where there are major differences. Do the contour lines form the same basic shapes and patterns? How accurate is the scale of your map? What about the distances between features? As you learn to read topo maps, you will start to see the contour lines in your mind's eye as you look at the landscape.

After you've spent some time reading topos in the field, try this exercise again.

Conclusion

Learning to read maps well takes practice, and there is no better way to practice than by being in the wilderness for an extended period of time. It is normal to struggle and to make mistakes sometimes. Navigating off-trail can be frustrating, but it will force you to develop your map skills. (Before jumping in over your head, however, read chapter 9 to learn how to avoid getting truly lost.)

The bottom line is: Don't get discouraged if you have trouble your first few times out. Be patient, and stick with it. You will soon develop an eye for wilderness terrain that will last you a lifetime.

CHAPTER 3 | FIXING YOUR POSITION

Terrain association is the foundational skill for locating yourself. It relies heavily on direct observation of your surroundings. The most successful terrain associators frequently, if not continuously, update their mental picture of where they are on the map. It is far easier to do this than to periodically establish a given position from scratch.

When terrain association breaks down, or if you have not been keeping up as you travel, you can locate yourself on the map using lines of position (LOPs). This is called fixing your position. LOPs, and the term *fix*, are borrowed from marine navigation, but the principles have long been in use on all forms of map and chart navigation.

Lines of Position

A line of position is an (often imaginary) line that can be visualized in the environment and also drawn on the map. A compass bearing is one type of line of position and can be reliably utilized in most situations. It is often faster, and can be more accurate, to utilize lines of position found in your environment—you just have to find them. Your map likely has many "built-in" lines of position that can be used to help locate yourself.

The key concept of a line of position is to visualize and draw a line that includes your current location. An accurate line of position dramatically reduces the number of positions where you might be. Instead of your likely position being "somewhere on this map," a line of position enables you to say that you are "somewhere on this line." As you add lines of position that simultaneously describe your location, you can narrow your position to a single point and know with certainty where you are. This is called a *position fix*.

A generalized method for drawing LOPs utilizes a transit. You can think of a transit as a sight line. A transit occurs when your position lines up with two other objects, such as islands. Islands are obvious markers, which is why this method works well in coastal navigation.

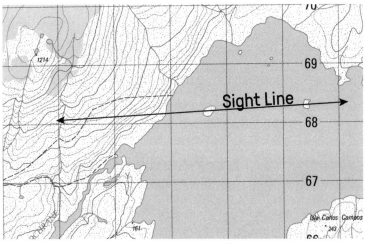

If you were somewhere on the slope on the northwest shore of this large lake, you might look out into the water and notice that two islands are visually "in line." If you draw that sight line on your map, you can securely know that your location must be somewhere along it.

The markers don't need to be islands, though. Any two distinctive objects that line up with where you are can be used to develop an LOP. Two peaks, for example:

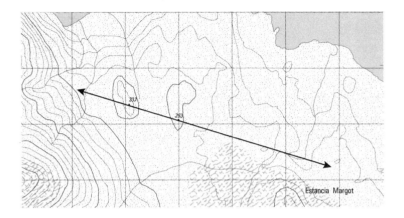

Use your imagination to draw LOPs on the map. This will help you to practice identifying features, as well as enable you to improvise LOPs when you really do need to know where you are with precision.

The idea of a straight line of position can be expanded to include lines that are "mostly" straight. Understand that "mostly" straight lines will give you a "mostly" accurate estimate of your position.

Some examples:

- **On a ridge:** Suppose you are hiking along a ridge, and you can say with certainty which ridge it is. That ridgeline is a LOP.

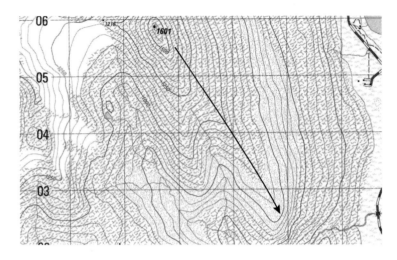

- **Looking along a ridge or a drainage:** The ridge can also be used to point along a LOP. Suppose you are hiking in an area where your position lines up with a nearby ridge. If the ridge continued, you'd be on it.

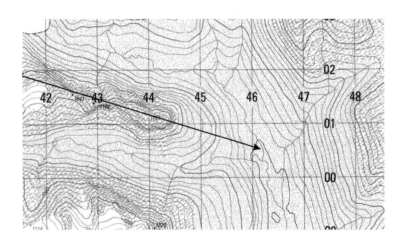

NOT ALL LOPS ARE STRAIGHT

The LOPs we've mentioned so far are (fairly) straight. Straight lines are easy to see and can be readily drawn on a map. But not all LOPs are straight. A curvy line can also work, but it is critical that the line can be accurately drawn on the map. Curvy lines are rarely developed from observation, but are rather identified as already-mapped features.

A classic example of an accurately mapped curvy line is a river. If you are standing on the south bank of a river, you know that you must be located on a thin blue line on your topo map. If you know which river you are on, you know which thin blue line to look at. Similarly, a major trail, a road, or a railroad track is an accurately marked curvy line on a map that can tell you where you are—provided you're standing on the trail/road/ track. Other "built-in" lines of position include power lines, shorelines of lakes or the ocean, or even the contour lines that describe topographic features.

TWO LOPS = POSITION FIX

Single lines of position are useful in narrowing down the zone you are in (e.g., "somewhere on this road"). That is good information to have, but it doesn't fix your location. The power of LOPs comes in combining two or more of them to narrow your position to a single point.

Suppose that you are standing on a trail, but didn't know where. The trail is a built-in LOP, and is marked as a black dashed line on the map. As you look out over the lake, you notice that two identifiable islands "line up" in your field of view. Draw that line on your map. You must be on that line also. In this example, there is only one location where the two lines cross. That's where you are.

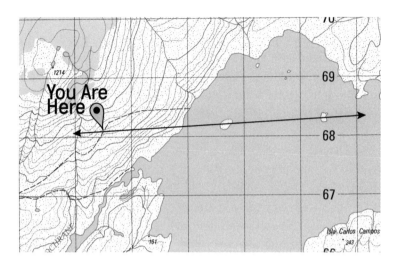

Any two reliable lines of position can be used to approximate your location. This example used a trail and a transit. In coastal navigation, island transits or transits between an island and a point are commonly used to develop lines of position. Other examples include:

- Two transits
- Two trails
- A transit and a shoreline
- A ridge and a trail

The combinations are limitless. The challenge comes in identifying transits and other LOPs that include your current location.

You can gain accuracy in fixing your location by adding lines of position. Your environment may not lend itself to "built-in" lines of position, but a compass can be used to draw accurate LOPs virtually anywhere. Compass bearings, and how they are used as lines of position, will be discussed later.

Zones

All of the example lines of position we've discussed are used in an attempt to pinpoint your location. LOPs can also be used to define zones where you aren't. Let's explore an analogy to clarify this: Suppose you've driven to a friend's house for dinner. When it's time to go home, you cannot find your car keys. You implicitly know that your keys are not at your own house, nor are they at your place of employment, nor are they in Venezuela (unless you have the good fortune to be dining with friends in Venezuela). You have automatically narrowed the zone of where your keys must be.

Now let's look at a navigation example in the backcountry: Suppose you started the day at a known location northeast of a major river and south of a major highway. As you move throughout the day, you can automatically exclude portions of the map where you know you are not. If you never cross a river (a natural LOP), you know that you're not southwest of that river's line on the map. If you never cross a paved highway (a built-in LOP), you know that you're not north of that line on the map. Provided that you have not crossed these two features, all of the area to the north is out of play, as are the areas southwest of the river. The zone of uncertainty is still sizable, but it is a much smaller space to place yourself as you associate terrain.

Note that this quick method only works if you:

- Know where you started, and you oriented the map before you set out.
- Keep track of important lines as you cross them (e.g., "Did we cross a river?").

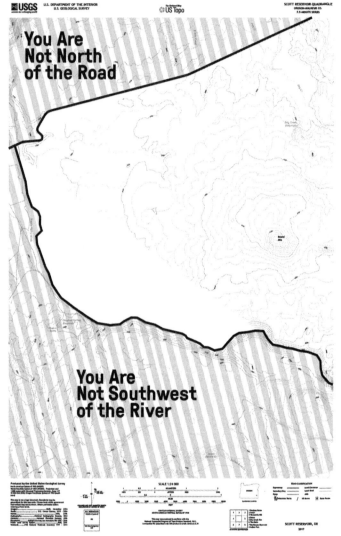

The zone of uncertainty

CHAPTER 4 | USING A COMPASS

Learning how to use a compass may seem needless in today's age of technology. However, gaining the knowledge to use one correctly can make your life easier, or even save it, as you hike in the backcountry.

Imagine that you've spent an exciting weekend in the mountains and are headed back to the trailhead when you get caught in the dark. There are several trails in the area, and when you finally reach one, you're not sure whether it's the right one, and if it is, whether you should go left or right. While you could look for terrain features during the day to help orient yourself, at night you can't see past the light of your headlamp. Anytime you find yourself in featureless terrain (desert, grasslands, tundra) or low-visibility situations (dense trees, fog, a whiteout), navigating by sun, stars, and terrain alone becomes difficult, and using a compass may be the only way to stay on track.

Once you have spent a few days in the field gaining a foundation in map reading with a topo map, you will be ready to add a compass to your navigation toolbox. In the case above, after trying to orient your map by memory, you would double-check your position with a compass and hopefully find that you are only a little off. Then, as you start down the trail, you would use the compass to verify the trail direction, eventually ending up at the trailhead.

A compass is a fantastic instrument, but becoming dependent on it can inhibit your development as a navigator. A GPS has greater power, and therefore poses an even greater risk of building your dependence and limiting your growth as a navigator. Be sure you know how to find your way in easy-to-read terrain, without a compass.

Your first few times in the field, only use your compass to double-check your map skills. (On thirty-day NOLS hiking courses in the Wyoming Rockies, students usually navigate for the first week or two using maps alone. Many NOLS sea kayak courses rely exclusively on terrain association for navigation.) Knowing when to use a compass, and when it is just a crutch, will come with time.

How a Compass Works (and Some Limitations)

The compass, as discussed in chapter 1, is an instrument that aligns its pointing needle with the ambient magnetic field. Most of the time, that field is the Earth's magnetic field. The compass can be influenced, however, by nearby objects, such as ferrous metals, magnets, and motors.

In the absence of "extra" magnetic influences, the Earth's magnetic field will dominate, and the compass will align itself to point toward the north and south magnetic poles of the Earth. This is useful because the Earth's magnetic field aligns *mostly* with the geodetic poles. The "mostly" is an important concept that we need to clear up before we begin navigating.

DECLINATION (VARIATION)

The magnetic North Pole and the geographic North Pole are not in the same place. The geographic (geodetic) North Pole is defined by the axis of rotation of the Earth. The geomagnetic North Pole is an artifact of the Earth's magnetic field, which is in slow but constant flux. The north magnetic pole is currently located in the northern Canadian Arctic near Ellesmere Island.

Potential Problems for Compass Users

Imagine that you are leading an early-season expedition across a high alpine mesa in a blizzard. You have been hiking in deep snow for over eight hours, visibility is down to about 10 feet, and some of the members in your party are starting to show signs of hypothermia. There is only one place on the mesa where you can hike down, and you will have to travel due south on a bearing for several miles to reach it. You face the direction that you believe to be south and double-check the direction with your compass. Several hard-fought hours later, you arrive at a massive cliff. A check of your map puts you about 2 miles off-course to the southwest, and 2 miles from camp. Some of your exhausted teammates are now discussing pushing you off the cliff.

What happened? Could there have been magnets sewn into your jacket? The idea might seem ridiculous; however, some jacket designers chose to use magnets, rather than Velcro, to seal the zipper's storm flap. In this case, a person could face any direction and believe that they were headed south, since the magnetic end of the needle would always point toward the jacket.

Much human-made gadgetry is magnetized. The easiest way to avoid falling prey to user compass errors is to double-check yourself. Better yet, have someone else double-check you. In any group outing, there should be at least two people working on navigation. Part of learning to be a good navigator is explaining your decisions and encouraging your teammates to challenge them.

The magnetic pole is mobile, and slowly moves relative to the Earth's surface.

The source of Earth's magnetism is thought to be the fluid movements in its molten core. As the core changes, so does the orientation and strength of the magnetic field, as it is measured on the surface of Earth.

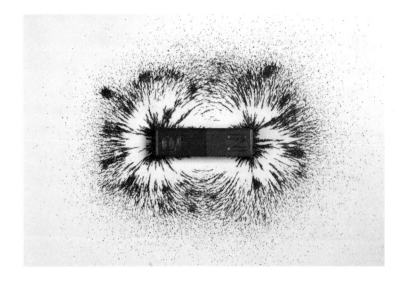

A simplified model of the magnetic field can approximate the effect for compass users. Imagine a large bar magnet (like the ones you used in your seventh-grade science class) that is the size of Earth and roughly aligned with the axis of rotation. The magnetic dipole is not exactly aligned (nor does it pass through the exact center of Earth), but is offset roughly 10 degrees from Earth's axis.

The resulting magnetic field (very) loosely approximates Earth's magnetic field. A compass on Earth will align itself with the field lines. Those field lines resemble the longitude lines on Earth, but they don't match up exactly. The difference between the two is the source of declination. Declination is the term for this concept when referring to a terrestrial map. In the nautical world, the same concept on a chart is called variation.

At the most fundamental level, the only thing that you need to understand is that your compass needle points to Ellesmere Island instead of the North Pole. Declination/variation is the angular difference between the two directions.

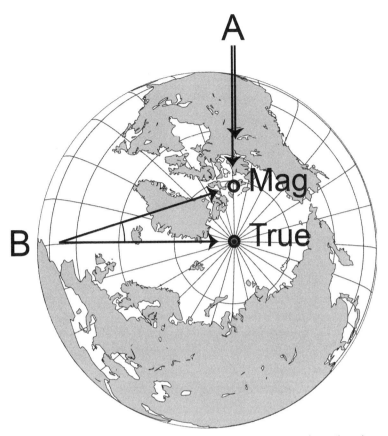

Declination/variation is the angular difference between magnetic north and true north.

Declination differs depending on your location. If you are in Wisconsin, Illinois, or Mississippi, your declination is close to zero, and you may not need to account for it. If you are in Seattle, your declination is about 19 degrees east, while in New York your declination is about 15 degrees west.

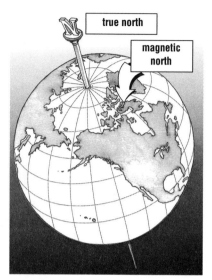

The needle of a compass does not point to the North Pole, but instead points to a location near Ellesmere Island, Canada.

To adjust for declination, use the meta information on your map or chart. On topographic maps, a declination diagram in the margin illustrates the difference between true and magnetic north.

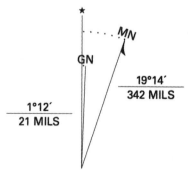

UTM GRID AND 2017 MAGNETIC NORTH DECLINATION AT CENTER OF SHEET

This example, taken from a USGS map for Holkham Bay, Alaska, shows magnetic north to be 19 degrees, 14 minutes east of north, as of 2017.

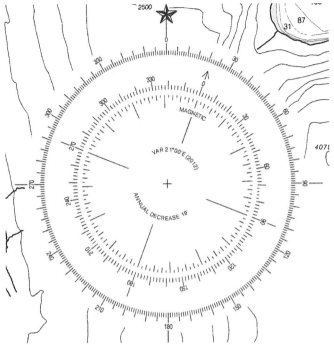

Compass rose taken from NOAA Chart 17311–Holkham Bay. The above image shows how declination (variation) is represented on nautical charts. This chart is from the same area around Holkham Bay, Alaska. It shows magnetic north to be 21 degrees east of north in 2012.

For the Mathematically Minded

Notice that the compass rose on the nautical chart indicates 21 degrees east of north in 2012. It also states that the variation decreases by 19 minutes every year. If we subtract the 1 degree, 35 minutes that this annual change represents over the five years between 2012 (the date of this chart) and 2017 (the date of the US topo), we get an estimated variation of 19 degrees, 25 minutes. This agrees with the 2017 declination stated on the US topo (19 degrees, 14 minutes).

Ignore the magnetic needle during this process. Start with the bezel set to north, so that it reads 0 degrees at the index line. Lay the compass over the declination diagram so that the star (representing the North Pole) is under the N on the bezel. Then, holding the base plate still, rotate the bezel until the orienting arrow is pointing to the MN on the diagram.

As a rule, if you are east of the 0-degree declination line, turn your bezel counterclockwise; if you are west, turn it clockwise. Declination is given in degrees east or west. Thus, although the index line will read 341 degrees in Seattle, the declination will be 19 degrees east. Folks with basic compasses may choose to mark their declination with a small triangular piece of colored tape on the base plate. This is worth doing if you will be traveling in one general area for an extended period of time, as it will help you turn the bezel in the right direction. If you are confused about which way to turn the dial, place your compass over the declination diagram.

All USGS quads have a declination diagram that allows you to reconcile magnetic north with true north. Place your compass over the diagram, matching the direction-of-travel arrow to true north and the orienting arrow to magnetic north. The standard topographic maps from other mapping agencies have a similar diagram—compass work with maps is fairly consistent the world over.

All nautical charts have at least one compass rose printed on them. Use this as the declination diagram with which to set your compass.

If you have a compass with a declination adjustment feature, adjust it by turning the tiny screw on the back of the bezel with the tiny screwdriver on your lanyard. Brunton compasses are adjusted by holding the bezel with one hand while pinching and rotating the housing with the other. In either case, the N on the azimuth ring should be at the index line, while the orienting arrow should point to the correct declination. If your compass features a dial for adjusting declination on the back of the bezel, remember that in the west you are dealing with east declination, and vice versa.

Not only is magnetic north constantly changing, but its rate of change is not uniform. The movement of magnetic north's position has been speeding up in the last decade. If your map is more than five years old, the declination indicated on it may be a little off. For areas in the United States, visit www.usgs.gov to get the most current declination for the area that you will be visiting.

While adjusting for declination can help in many navigation challenges, it is not the factor that influences accuracy the most. Adjustments in declination due to drift are rarely more than a couple of degrees, even for maps decades old. This small amount matters in some situations, but more often it doesn't. Commercial compasses can have an accuracy of +/- 2 degrees. This is called *instrument error*. Procedural errors are added to this (i.e., how carefully measurements are made). Chances are that sub-degree corrections from magnetic drift are much smaller than the accumulated error when using a compass in the field.

BOXING THE NEEDLE

After setting your declination, you can use your compass to face true north. You accomplish this by boxing the needle—moving the compass until the magnetic end of the needle is outlined by the orienting arrow. There are two ways to box the needle: by holding the base plate in place while turning the bezel, or by rotating the entire compass (base plate and all) without touching the bezel. Try both ways a few times to make sure that you understand the difference.

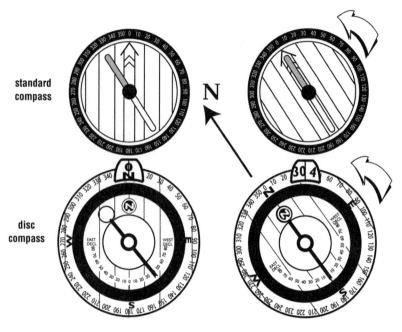

Boxing the needle

The second method is the one to use for finding true north. Set the compass declination, and then box the needle by rotating the entire compass. The direction-of-travel arrow on the base plate is now pointing to true north.

Orienting a Map with a Compass

Orienting a map to the land features around you using terrain association is the best way to practice your map-reading skills. Try to orient your map to the land every time you look at it in the field, and learn how to use a compass to double-check your orientation or to orient the map when you cannot see land features.

First, set the declination for your location. Next, lay your map on a flat surface or hold it so that it is level. Place your compass on the map so that the base plate runs along either the left or right margin and the direction-of-travel arrow is pointing north—to the top of the map. Then, box the needle by rotating the map without disturbing the compass base plate. Your map is now oriented to the surrounding landscape.

With some maps, you can also place your compass over the declination diagram and rotate the map until the needle is aligned with the magnetic north vector. This method can only be used on maps with a declination diagram.

Bearings

Bearings are directions given in degrees between 0 and 360. You can think of them as more precise versions of the cardinal directions. To follow a bearing, first write it down on your map. Then turn the dial so that the bearing appears at the index line, and box the needle by holding the compass steady and turning your body. The direction-of-travel arrow should now be pointing along the bearing, toward your new objective. If you have a compass with a mirror and a sight, now is the time to use it.

Pick out a distinct landmark (such as an unusually shaped boulder or a particularly tall tree) that lies directly along your bearing, between you and your objective. Walk to the landmark, and repeat the process, choosing another landmark on the same bearing, until you arrive at your destination. Try to choose features that are within sight but are as far away as possible.

Going around large obstacles, such as a cliff or a lake, on your bearing can be tricky. There are two ways to do it. The first

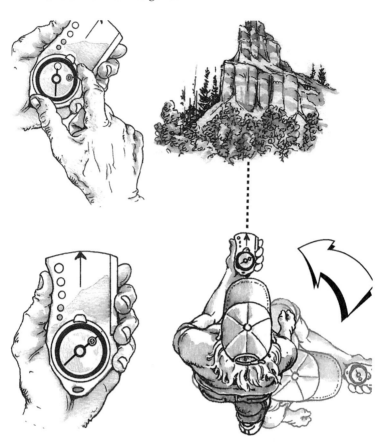

To follow a bearing, dial the bezel until the bearing appears at the index line, and turn your body to box the needle. You can then follow the bearing to your destination.

way is to sight beyond the obstacle. Say that you need to go around a lake, for example. You would sight an intermediate on the other side of the lake, put the compass away, walk around the lake to your landmark, and start again. This is the fastest and most accurate method.

If you can't see a good intermediate past the obstacle, walk left or right in a perpendicular line away from the bearing until

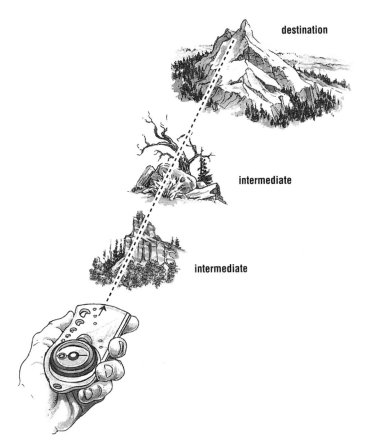

Use intermediate landmarks that lie along your bearing to help keep you moving in the right direction.

you can pass the obstacle. Count the number of steps that you take away from the bearing, then walk forward, past the obstacle, following the direction-of-travel arrow so that you are walking parallel to the original bearing. When you've cleared the obstacle, count the same number of steps back to your bearing. While it may sometimes be your only option, this practice is time-consuming, prone to error, and best avoided.

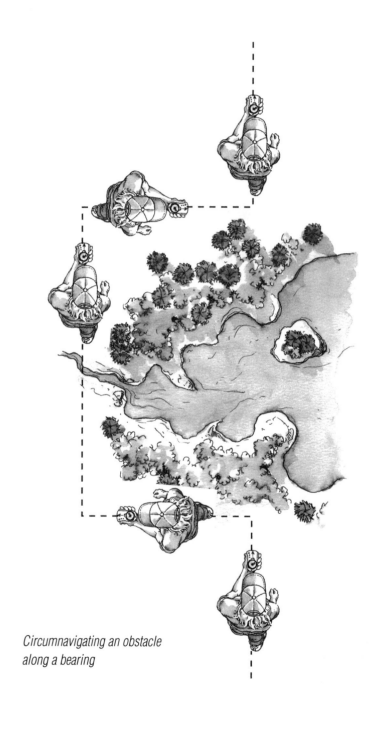

Circumnavigating an obstacle along a bearing

For those who work on search-and-rescue teams, or compete in adventure races or other competitive navigation events, following a bearing quickly and accurately is the key to success. Practice jogging from intermediate to intermediate without ever stopping completely. Try looking at your compass while you are moving. Brunton and Suunto make orienteering thumb compasses that attach to your wrist and thumb. These can be read

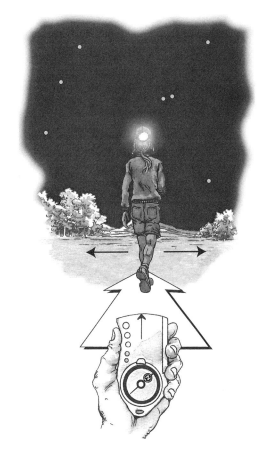

One technique for following a bearing in the dark is to have someone wear a headlamp and sight them as they walk forward. You can direct them left and right as needed.

on the fly. If you need to move quickly, a thumb compass can serve as an excellent backup to your base plate compass.

If you find yourself trying to follow a bearing in the dark or without adequate landmarks, you have a couple of options. One is to march along with your eyes on the compass, following the direction-of-travel arrow while keeping the needle boxed. The second, more accurate (but slower), option is to have a teammate walk ahead and take bearings on them. If it is dark, have them wear a second headlamp backward. They should begin by walking about 50 feet in front of your team. As they move forward, sight them every minute or so and give verbal directions ("Move right five steps," for example) to keep them on the bearing. The team should then walk toward them, repeating the process until the destination is reached.

TAKING A BEARING FROM TERRAIN

There are many reasons you may need to take a bearing from the terrain. Imagine that you can see your objective, a distant peak. However, a heavily forested valley lies between you and that peak. You realize that, as you descend into the valley, you will lose sight of the peak and could get off route. By taking a bearing on the peak before descending, you set your compass to guide you through the valley in a straight line toward the peak. You can follow the bearing until you emerge from the trees and can see land features again.

To take a bearing from the terrain, hold your compass at chest level directly in front of you, pointing the direction-of-travel arrow at your objective. Then, while holding the base plate level, rotate the bezel to box the needle. Your bearing is the number on the azimuth ring at the index line.

If your compass has a sighting mirror, you can precisely sight your objective at eye level using the gunsight notch on the top of the mirror. Adjust the mirror so that you can see the bezel well enough to box the needle while the base plate is level. The gunsight, the centerline dividing the mirror, and the peep sight all need to line up on your objective. As you take the bearing, imagine a laser beam coming out from between your eyes, through the compass sights, and continuing all the way to your destination.

TAKING A BEARING FROM A MAP

Sometimes you can't see your objective to take a bearing on it. What would you do if, in the previous example, it got dark once you were in the forested valley and you had forgotten to take a terrain bearing? What if a storm blew in? In situations like this, if you have been keeping track of where you are on the map, hope is not lost. All you need to know is where your current location and your objective are on the map.

There are several ways to take a bearing from a map. A simple and accurate method is to orient the map with your compass, then line up the base plate along the imaginary line between your location and your objective, with the direction-of-travel arrow pointed toward your objective. This line can be drawn on the map. While holding the base plate on the line, turn the dial until the needle is boxed, then read your bearing at the index line.

If you are accustomed to taking a bearing using grid lines on a map, continue to do so. Done correctly, either method can be effective, but they cannot hybridize. To reduce the likelihood of mistakes, find what works best for you, and be consistent.

PLOTTING A BEARING ONTO A MAP

By reversing the process for taking a bearing from a map, you can plot a bearing onto a map. This skill is useful for locating yourself or identifying a distant land feature on the map. If you keep up with your current location on the map (like a good navigator), you will rarely need to plot a bearing to locate yourself. Nonetheless, it can take years to develop an eye for distinguishing similar land features that lie in the same general direction. Being able to plot bearings can help with this.

Let's say you know your current location on the map, but are having trouble distinguishing between several peaks to the northeast. After orienting your map and marking your current location on it, take a field bearing on the landmark you wish to locate. Once you've established the bearing, don't touch the dial. Next, place a bottom corner of the base plate on your current location so that the direction-of-travel arrow is pointing away from it and toward your objective. Hold the corner there while rotating the base plate until the needle is boxed. Then, draw a line from your location along the edge of the compass and across the map. If your compass has a mirror, open it to give the compass a longer edge. If you still need to extend the line past the compass, you can do some creative map folding and use the map as a straightedge. In any case, provided the

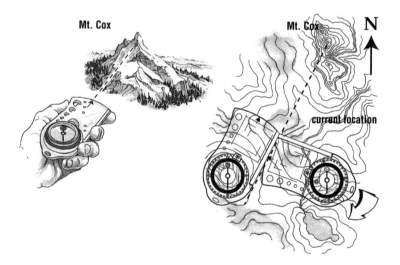

Transferring a bearing onto a map: take a bearing on a landmark, place a corner of the compass on your destination, and rotate it until the needle is boxed.

line is long enough, the landmark in question will lie somewhere along it.

BACK BEARINGS

If you have to go a particularly long distance on a bearing, consider taking a back bearing. To do so, turn around so that you are facing directly away from your objective. You can tell that you are facing the right direction when you have boxed the

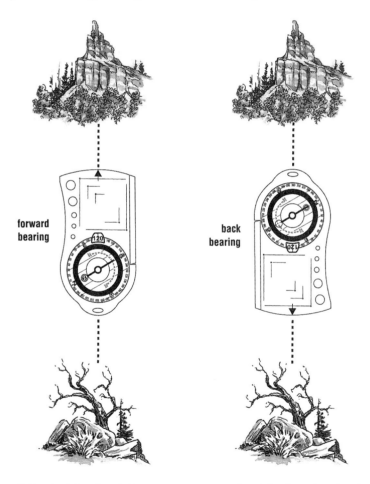

forward
bearing

back
bearing

Taking back bearings helps you stay on route when following a long bearing.

south-seeking end of the needle. Be sure to rotate your body and the compass—without touching the dial. Then, find a large, distinct landmark that lies directly in front of you.

Turn around and begin traveling toward your objective. Stop occasionally to turn and box the south-seeking end of the needle. The direction-of-travel arrow should be pointing directly toward your starting point, the landmark beyond it, and any other intermediate landmarks you've passed so far. If these elements are not aligned, you have strayed from the bearing.

COMPASS-BEARING LOPS

By plotting a bearing onto a map, you've created a line of position that passes through the sighted object. If that LOP can be crossed with any other reliable LOP, you can fix your position.

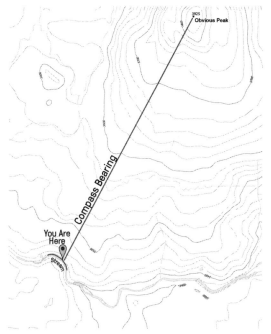

Compass bearing from Obvious Peak crossed with stream

FIXING YOUR POSITION USING BEARINGS

A common practice in wilderness navigation is to fix your position using only bearings. For navigators who have practiced compass bearings and can perform them quickly, a fix using only compass LOPs is fast and accurate.

If you can positively identify three or more visible land features, you can plot bearings to them. This self-locating method

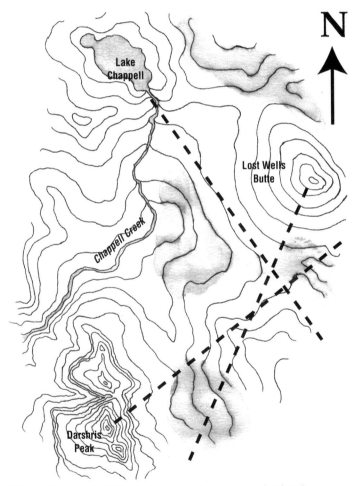

Triangulation entails taking bearings on three separate landmarks.

is known as triangulation. We use three bearings, rather than two, because it adds accuracy. The landmarks should be spaced evenly around you—more than 60 degrees is ideal.

After orienting your map, take field bearings on each landmark, just as you would using the linear feature method. Draw straight lines along the compass edge for each bearing, extending the line on either side of the landmark. If you are perfectly accurate, the three lines will meet at a point. This level of accuracy is rare in the field, however; more often, the three lines intersect to form a small triangle (this triangle is called a "cocked hat"). A point inside of this triangle is the best approximation of your location.

The more accurate your bearings, the smaller the triangle will be. It is important to note, however, that your true location is not guaranteed to be inside this triangle. While the fix is taken to be the geometric center of the triangle, there is a zone of uncertainty surrounding that fix, and the zone is not bound by the triangle.

If you find yourself needing to triangulate often, you might need to work on your terrain association skills and/or increase your awareness of your location as you travel. Think of triangulation as a backstop to reestablish your position so that you can use terrain association once again.

Each extra line takes time and energy to plot and has diminishing returns in terms of adding accuracy. A common practice is to cross three lines of position. This provides an economical balance of accuracy and effort.

Using a Map and Compass Outside North America

If you will be traveling in wilderness areas outside the United States, there are some important things to know. Maps from elsewhere may not adhere to USGS norms for scale, units, symbology, or even colors. Topographic maps of a 1:24,000 or 1:25,000 scale may not be available. You may be able to find maps at only 1:100,000 scale, for example. Most mapping agencies outside of the United States use metric (meters and kilometers) rather than statute (feet and miles) units of measurement for distance and elevation.

You may also need a different compass. The Earth's magnetic fields pull compass needles not only in cardinal directions, but also up and down. ("Up" and "down" being relative to the surface of the Earth. It might be more descriptive to say "inward" and "skyward.") The magnetic pole toward which a compass points is subterranean, so as you travel toward the Arctic, your needle will point toward this underground location. The details get more complicated as you travel to the southern hemisphere, where the needle points toward the pole but is not tangent to the Earth. This phenomenon is called *compass dip*. If the dip is too great, the needle will drag on the top or bottom of the housing and will not spin freely.

Compass makers divide the Earth into several magnetic dip zones and balance compass needles differently for each zone. Therefore, a compass purchased in Ontario may not be useful in helping you to find a volcano in Fiji. Contact your compass manufacturer directly to make sure that your compass will work in the zone to which you are headed. You can purchase a compass with a global pivot that is uniquely balanced to work in any magnetic dip zone. Wherever you go, be sure to double-check that your compass works well in a local town before heading into the backcountry.

Exercises

Exercise 1: Taking and Following a Bearing on a Landmark

Start in a familiar location, whether urban or rural. Take a moment to orient yourself, finding your local declination and setting it on your compass. Which way is true north? Is it where you expected it to be? Let your mind associate what your compass is telling you about the land around you.

Then take a bearing on a water tower, tall hill, or other large, faraway, visible landmark. Use your compass to follow the bearing toward the landmark. Stop every 100 meters or so and take a back bearing. Are you still on track?

Repeat this process three more times, sighting landmarks and following bearings in each cardinal direction.

Exercise 2: Off-Trail Loop Hike on Bearings

This exercise could take three to eight hours, depending on the distance and terrain you select. It requires 15 to 20 minutes of map work before hiking. If you have friends joining you on the hike, you may want to do part A at home in advance.

If you are hopelessly city-locked and have a map of the right scale, you can practice the skills in this exercise (and exercise 3) in an urban setting, taking bearings on buildings and so forth. However, just as immersion is the best way to learn a foreign language, nothing will improve your ability to navigate in the wilderness better than navigating in the wilderness.

Before heading into the field, make sure you have gained some map-reading experience on-trail and are comfortable with your survival skills in case you become lost or injured. It is a good idea to take a friend or two, particularly if you are new to the backcountry. Don't forget to leave a travel plan and pack a lunch and essential gear.

Part A: Planning the Route

Begin by setting the declination, orienting your map, and marking the location of your starting point (often called the trailhead on your way into the wilderness, and the roadhead on your way out), then pick at least three recognizable landmarks to which you could hike. Your goal is to plan a loop hike that visits all three landmarks. We'll call these landmarks your "waypoints." They can be ponds, small hills, drainage confluences, trail intersections, or railroad or power line crossings. These landmarks should be at least 1 mile apart and visible from a short distance and from one another—hilltops, for example.

Mark the waypoints clearly on the map and number them 1, 2, and 3.

Pencil in your route on the map. Chapter 5 covers route planning in depth, but for now your main concern should be making things as simple as possible. As you plan your route, measure the total distance and elevation gain. Is the distance realistic for your party? Write down your estimated return time in the margin of the map, keeping in mind that off-trail travel is slower than on-trail travel. If your route is excessively long, full of obstacles, or likely to leave you out after dark, it is probably too complicated for this exercise.

If the route is manageable, write down your estimated times of arrival (ETAs) next to each waypoint. Plot bearings on the map from point to point in the order that you wish to follow them, making sure that the direction-of-travel arrow is pointed in the direction that you will be traveling each time. Write the bearing beside each line you've drawn to remind you where to set your bezel at each waypoint. Double-check that the bearings you've plotted do not go over any cliffs or large bodies of water that you can't circumnavigate.

Part B: Following the Route

Over time, you will be able to decide whether to follow a bearing or to use your map based on your judgment of the terrain, visibility, and so on. For the purposes of this exercise, try to follow your route from point to point, using your map as little as possible. Focus instead on route finding and staying on each compass bearing.

If you need to sight intermediate landmarks as you follow the bearings, do so at the greatest distance possible. Also, sight each waypoint from time to time as you approach it. Is it on the same bearing that you are following?

If you start out on a bearing and seem to be going in the wrong direction, stop and reorient your map to check that you haven't plotted it incorrectly. Because you have your bearings written down, you can readjust your bezel to orient the map whenever necessary. Just be sure to reset the bearing when you are finished.

Keep track of your pace. Are you meeting your ETAs? Have you passed your waypoint? Is there a visible feature that will tell you if you've gone too far?

Once you've successfully traveled from your third waypoint to your starting point, congratulate yourself—you've just planned and followed your own off-trail route! What worked well? Where did you run into trouble? If you struggled with the exercise, consider practicing plotting bearings at home and then trying again in another area.

Exercise 3: Using Bearings to Locate Your Position

This exercise should take from a couple of hours to a full day, depending on the location you choose to do your triangulating. The key to success in this exercise is planning well in advance and choosing a good spot with lots of recognizable landmarks. The more land features there are, the better. (If you can't visit an area with enough topographic relief to sight landmarks from a distance, don't drive yourself crazy trying to take bearings on landmarks that you can't identify. Instead, save this exercise for a trip to the mountains or canyons.)

Spend some time looking at maps in advance, and ask others for advice if you aren't sure where to go. Most outdoor retailers can recommend good day hikes in their area. You will need fairly good weather in order to see distant landmarks. Plan to leave early and on a day without precipitation or fog. Once again, consider bringing one or more friends and doing your route planning in advance.

Part A: Planning the Route

Choose an area with distinct land features that you can pick out on the map and easily identify on land. Remember, if you can't positively identify at least two landmarks, you can't use bearings to find your location. An ideal spot for this exercise is an open valley with high ridges on both sides.

Mark a small triangle on your map in the place where you plan to do your triangulation. We'll call this your turnaround point. Pencil in the route from the roadhead to the turnaround point. If your route follows a trail or drainage, it will be quicker and easier to follow and you will have a linear reference point, which will make it possible to determine your location from a single bearing.

Part B: Following the Route

As you hike toward the turnaround point, identify up to five land features that you can positively locate on the map. Try to use features at different distances and directions from the route that you are following.

Each time you can sight another feature, stop and try to identify your exact location using terrain association. Then, double-check your accuracy by locating your position with bearings. How did you do?

Once you arrive at your turnaround point, you are ready to practice triangulation. Can you positively identify the land features that you were expecting to see when you looked at your map? Mark your location using terrain association only. Now, triangulate. How large is the triangle created by your bearings? Is it close to the position that you estimated?

On the hike back, stop in different places and take bearings on some of the features that you sighted on your way in.

Conclusion

If you've spent some time doing these exercises, you are well on your way to having competent compass skills. Keep things in perspective, however. Think of the compass as an essential piece of equipment in your navigation toolbox, but one that ranks third behind your brain and a good map.

PLANNING A ROUTE

In wilderness navigation, good route-finding means planning and following an efficient route—one that balances speed, safety, and energy conservation. The difficulty of the route must match the abilities of the party. Terrain association skills will be put to work during planning: recognizing hazards, terrain types, and steepness of the ground over which you will travel. Effective planning requires seeing the route in your mind's eye before you arrive.

Lessons Learned

by Darran Wells

In 2002, I was leading a team in the Eco-Challenge Expedition Race. On the second day, I decided to take the team up and over a steep ridge in order to shave about 10 miles off a 40-mile trek through dense Fijian rainforest. As is often the case, there was no way to tell from the maps where the forest density changed. After six hours of steep bushwhacking through brutal vines and bamboo, we reached the top of the narrow ridge. A series of short vertical drops over a mile-long, 60-degree slope covered in loose rock and vegetation lay ahead. We were out of water and needed to get to the river at the bottom quickly, so we headed down.

As we slid, fell, and climbed our way down the slope, vines and small trees pulled loose. Cliffs forced us to reroute five times. At different points, two of my teammates fell 20 to 30 feet; had they not been wearing helmets, they could have been critically injured. By the time we made it to the river, we had dropped from 15th to 40th place. The other teams, who had followed the river, covered more ground but were able to do so at a steady pace with few route-finding challenges. Not only were they ahead, they hadn't taken unnecessary risks and wasted valuable energy.

The navigation mistakes that I made in Fiji are common when planning and following an off-trail route. Here they are one by one:

1. The route was not appropriate for the entire team. I was the only rock climber on the team and I chose a route that was too steep and did not take into account my teammates' experience and desires. The small-scale (1:100,000) maps we had were not detailed enough to show short cliffs. I should have erred on the side of caution.

2. There were no easily identifiable handrails for long sections of the route, which forced us to travel by compass bearings alone in dense jungle for many hours.

3. There were no water sources on the route I chose.

4. We were too inexperienced with that environment (Fijian jungle) to accurately predict how dense the brush would be, and how slow the bushwhacking might be. Consequently, my time estimates were wrong.

5. When it started to get rough, we kept pushing on, instead of turning back for the longer but easier route.

I knew not to do these things, and had even taught others not to do them. How is it that we can make the same navigational mistakes again and again? It's similar to the way that people become addicted to gambling. "What if it really pays off this time?" you say to yourself. The temptation to find a secret shortcut and to be a navigation hero can be strong. If you are leading others, however, you owe it to them to ask yourself what is motivating you to choose the routes you do. What are the risks and potential consequences? Consult the others in your group. Make conservative decisions when potential losses are significant.

If the situation starts to look challenging, stop and seriously consider turning back. There is no such thing as "lost time." Every time you double back, you learn a valuable lesson. Be willing to accept that you may not have chosen the best route for that group on that day. If you are going to turn back, it's best to make that decision as soon as possible. Mistakes are part of navigation. Forget the blame and shame—just turn around and get going in the right direction. Others in your group may complain about turning back, but those complaints are nothing compared to unplanned nights out, hospital bills, or worse.

Gaining Access

Before you get too detailed in your route planning, you should first determine if you are allowed to be in the area where you hope to travel. In the United States, public lands are plentiful, and access is typically straightforward. The use of public lands may be regulated or managed, however. Some areas require permits. Some activities may be prohibited in one type of managed land (for example, mountain biking is not permitted in wilderness areas) but encouraged in others. Land use regulations in other jurisdictions may be more complex than those in the United States.

Your first step in planning a land route is to identify the type of lands that you'll be using. Will you be on public lands? Which agency manages the land, and what are their requirements for access? Within the United States, the largest public land managers are the Bureau of Land Management, the National Park Service, the National Forest Service, and the

Fish and Wildlife Service. Each of these agencies has a different mandate, so they manage for different priorities. Recreational access is not always at the top of the list.

Outside of the United States, you will have to explore the local jurisdiction's bureaucracy, and locate the corresponding manager for the area(s) that you wish to use.

Not all wild and beautiful places are in the public domain. If your route crosses private land, you should gain permission to pass from the landowner.

For water routes (sea kayaking, SUP, etc.), access is often easier. Waterways are considered essential transportation corridors in many cultures, so access is often open. Getting to the put-in, however, can be a sticking point. Legal access to and from the water route must be conducted in the same way as for an all-land route, and permission from the landowner or manager may be required.

Choosing a Route

After you've determined your objective, start designing your route by looking at maps and locating places with vehicle access. Will you leave a vehicle somewhere and return to that same spot? Will someone drop you off and/or pick you up? Will you leave a car at another trailhead?

If your route includes off-trail travel, keep in mind the price that you will pay in time and energy. Traveling off-trail usually takes longer and is more tiring than hiking on a trail. The exception to this may be travel in open meadows, desert, or snow-covered areas; on ice or large rock slabs; or in open areas where the surface is not much different than that of a trail. Off-trail travel often requires you to deal with hazards that a trail might avoid, such as exposure to lightning, steep snow or ice, rocks and boulders, downed trees, fast-moving water, and/or dense vegetation. As you plan an off-trail route, build in plenty of extra time to recover from setbacks.

Being able to judge when and when not to head away from the trail is the mark of a good navigator. Some of the most beautiful wilderness areas do not have trails. There will also be times when it is to your advantage to travel off-trail to shorten the distance to your objective.

If you'll be going through mountainous areas, remember that more trees usually indicates a more stable slope. In North America, north-facing slopes tend to be more thickly vegetated and have snow longer than in other aspects, which is good for skiing and ice climbing but bad for hiking and biking. In any given mountain range, the snow line, tree line, and tundra zones should appear at about the same elevation throughout.

If your trip will take more than a day, you'll need to plan where to camp along the route. Your first thought in choosing a campsite should be safety. Is the campsite close to a steep slope that could avalanche or release falling rocks? Are there dead trees that could fall on your tent if the wind picks up? Upstream weather can cause unexpected rises in river levels and flooding in canyon country—is the area subject to flash flooding? Is it exposed to the wind and weather? What is a reasonable distance for your group to hike on a given day? Consider planning alternate campsites that are easier to reach in case you can't make it to your primary campsite.

If you want to avoid crowds, seek advice from land managers about less-visited areas and quieter times to visit. Choose a durable surface to camp, such as pine duff, sand, snow, a rocky slab, or a non-vegetated area. With proper planning, you can camp comfortably on almost any flat surface. Plan your campsites so that they are at least 200 feet from water. This will decrease the impact on overused areas and leave the water accessible to wildlife. Even if you're not planning to camp, your hiking group should be self-sufficient and have all of the necessary gear to survive overnight. This allows folks to relax when navigating, knowing that if they can't find the way, camping is an option, and they can continue in the morning.

On-Trail Travel

All trails are not created equal. They can vary dramatically depending on the terrain, the season, who built them, how they are maintained, and for whom they were originally designed. Some have mile markers and signs at every intersection, while others are unmarked, except at the trailhead.

Trails can be marked in several different ways. Some trails are indicated by blazes—slash marks made in trees with an ax or machete at about 4 to 6 feet from the ground. The phrase "blazing trails" comes from pioneers who originally marked trees to establish trails through western forests. In national forests in the United States, trees are usually blazed with a short slash mark below a longer slash mark, like an upside-down letter *i*. On well-blazed trails, each blaze is visible from the one before it. Trees are often blazed on both sides so that they can be recognized from either direction. In forested areas where blazes are used, however, there are often animals (bears and elk, for example) that commonly rub or scratch trees, which removes the bark from them. A little time in the field will make it easier for you to recognize the difference between a long, symmetrical blaze and an animal sign.

In order to better preserve trailside trees, some land managers are now using metallic tags to mark a trail rather than blazes. Others paint a blaze on the tree rather than cutting into the bark.

Another way to tell if you're on-trail in a forest is by looking for log cuts. Those who build and maintain trails cut fallen trees to clear a path. These cut trees sit on the sides of maintained

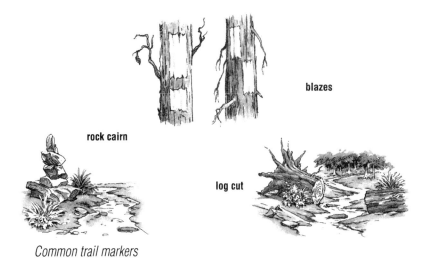

Common trail markers

trails and are easy to distinguish from trees that have fallen naturally.

In treeless areas, rock cairns are often built to keep folks on the trail. Cairns are rocks piled up between knee and waist high. They are a simple way to stay on the trail, but they can become a visual nuisance in high-traffic areas. Cairns are unnecessary in areas where the trail is easy to follow.

Have you ever followed a trail that seemed to disappear? There are several reasons why this happens. Animals routinely use human-made trails to move from place to place in the wilderness. However, while we build in switchbacks and turns to prevent erosion and to make the trail easier to hike or ride, animals are not that interested in switchbacks. It is not uncommon to see game trails that continue on where the human-made trail makes a sharp turn. If there is enough animal traffic, and you are not anticipating a turn in the trail, it becomes easy to miss your turn and continue on a game trail that will eventually disappear. Be mindful of trails that make sudden direction changes. When the trail seems to narrow suddenly, or the trail surface changes, stop and take a look around. Are you missing a turn? Did you just start heading up or down a hill? Is there a switchback covered in snow?

If you are trying to follow a trail but are not sure you are on it, stop and look back. Are you able to find your way back to the trail? In hilly areas, it's easy to meander downhill and off the trail. If you were traversing along a hill when you lost the trail, chances are good that the trail is above you. People tend to take the path of least resistance and head downhill when they are feeling lost or having difficulty following a trail.

You should either be on the trail or off the trail. Never walk beside trails or cut switchbacks, which causes erosion.

Off-Trail Travel

Following an off-trail route is usually more challenging than moving along a trail, but there are some techniques that you can use to make navigation easier. Try taking advantage of long view corridors when traveling in heavily forested areas. A see, or shot, is the distance that is visible in a given direction from where you are standing. If you are traveling off-trail in a forest or jungle, move along the longest see in the general direction that you want to travel. When you come to the end of the see, repeat the process until you reach your objective or a more open area. The first and second person should be communicating and keeping the whole group moving in the right direction.

The first things to look for when planning an off-trail route are handrails, also known as line features. A handrail is a linear land feature that parallels your route. You may walk right next to it, or it may be visible from a distance, but as you travel, you should be able to see it from time to time. If you maintain a constant distance between yourself and a straight handrail, you know that you are traveling in a straight line. Cliffs, ridges,

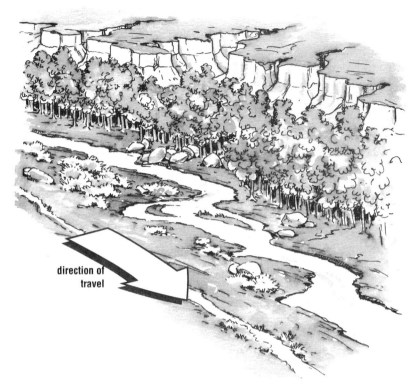

direction of
travel

Handrails, such as rivers or cliffs, make it relatively easy to move in a straight line.

drainages, shorelines, fences, power lines, and train tracks all make good handrails. (You can handrail roads or trails, but why not just walk on them if you can see them?) While you will rarely be able to follow the same handrail from your origin to your destination, there is often some feature that you can handrail for at least a leg of the journey.

One way to better reach an objective that lies on a linear feature, like a trail, is by intentionally aiming off from your objective. Say you are traveling off-trail and you need to locate a trail intersection. If you head directly for it, unless your navigation is perfect, chances are good that you will wind up intersecting the trail somewhere to the left or right of the inter-section. Which way do you go? If you don't have great visibility, you have only a 50 percent chance of heading the right way. By purposefully aiming a few degrees off from the proper bearing, you will know which side of the objective you are on, and which way you need to travel.

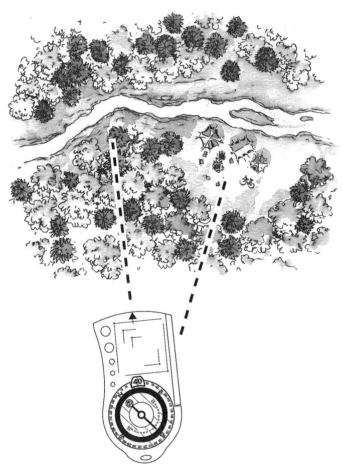

An example of aiming off: Here, the navigator intentionally aims a little off from her target so that she can follow the river to camp.

Another critical tool for navigating off-trail is using what are known as catching features or backstops. Any feature that lies beyond your objective and is more or less perpendicular to your route can be a backstop. It needs to be something that you can recognize so that you will know when you've gone too far and passed your objective. A river, lake, fence line, mountain, canyon, road, trail, or any other obvious large feature will work. If possible, you should always have a backstop in mind as you travel off-trail. Ask yourself, "How will I know if I overshoot my objective?"

Points along your route at which you leave a trail or handrail are called attack points. They should be easily recognizable; ask yourself, "How will I know when to leave the trail?" Good attack points include trail intersections and the places where a trail crosses a drainage or tree line.

Special Travel Considerations When Route Planning

STEEP TERRAIN

Mountaineers use rating systems to describe how steep and difficult a route up a mountain may be. These systems provide a common language for climbers and hikers to discuss the difficulty of a route. North American climbers generally use the Yosemite Decimal System (YDS). In the YDS, there are five classes of terrain:

- **Class 1:** Simple walking. City sidewalks and most trails are class 1 terrain.
- **Class 2:** Steep hiking on-trail or off-trail. Most class 2 terrain is found in mountains or canyons.
- **Class 3:** Scrambling. You may need to use your hands occasionally. Steep boulder fields are an example of class

Class 1

Class 2

Class 3

Class 4

Class 5

The Yosemite Decimal System

3 terrain. There is the potential for short falls. Some people choose to carry a rope.

- **Class 4:** Simple climbing where falls can be fatal but are unlikely. Many people will use ropes.
- **Class 5:** Rock climbing. Climbing class 5 terrain should involve the use of a rope, belaying, and other specific climbing techniques. Climbers subdivide this class into difficulty ratings from 5.0 to 5.15.

Unless you are properly trained in rock climbing and are prepared to climb, class 4 and class 5 terrain should be avoided. In the previously described misadventure in Fiji, the descending group was in class 4 terrain, unroped—a potentially critical mistake. Class 3 terrain is slow going, and is also best avoided in most cases.

There are certainly situations where you may be tempted to shorten a route by traveling through steep terrain. Occasionally, it is significantly faster to go up and over a steep ridge than to walk all the way around it. Before heading into steep terrain, ask yourself these questions:

- What are the risks and hazards of going up and over? What is the weather doing? Do we have enough water? Is there a danger of falling rocks?
- What is the energy cost of going over the hill? Will we still have the time and the energy to make it to our objective on schedule?
- Could it actually be slower for this group to go over the top?
- Will the route-finding be harder or easier?

BOULDERS, TALUS, SCREE, AND TILL

As a mountain erodes, fields of broken-down rocks form on its sides. These rock fields can be divided into categories, depending on the size of the individual rock chunks.

The largest chunks are boulders. These can range in size from the size of an ice chest (the kind you might use to keep drinks cold at the beach) to a large house. Boulder fields are tedious and dangerous. Traveling through large boulders is slow and requires good balance, and occasionally some rudimentary rock-climbing skills. Avoid boulder fields whenever possible.

Talus ranges in size from a small ice chest down to the size of a softball. While traveling on talus is not pleasant, it is usually not as time-consuming and energy-draining as traveling on boulders. When talus is on a steep slope, however, there is the danger of someone above knocking a rock down on those below. It's nice to have shoes or boots that protect your ankles from loose rocks when traveling on talus.

Scree includes any rock smaller than a softball but larger than a grain of sand. Scree fields can make a fantastic descent route if you wear gaiters to prevent the pebbles from getting into your boots. Going up a scree field is an entirely different story, however. Depending on the shape of the scree, you may create a small avalanche with each step that you take. At times, ascending a scree slope feels like taking two steps backwards for every one step forward. Doing an ascending traverse can also be slow going on scree.

In mountainous areas carved by glaciers, you may come across glacial till. Till consists of bits of rock the size of sand grains, or smaller, that have been ground up by glaciers. Walking on till is like walking on a beach that has been tilted up and dropped on the side of a mountain. It can be slow going, but is generally not as slow to ascend as scree or boulders.

The most efficient routes usually stick to open terrain. Open terrain is easy to walk on, and it allows you to see greater distances and make navigational decisions earlier.

THICK VEGETATION

Typically, ridges are less vegetated and offer better visibility than drainages. Drainages are often choked with vegetation that thrives on the water available there. Some of the nastier varieties of trees and shrubbery to travel through are thick bamboo in jungles, alders on steep slopes in western North America, marsh willows in the Rockies, countless thorny vines in the tropics, and manzanita and cat's claw in the southwestern United States. Cacti can be rough in the desert, but are more easily avoided. As you develop an eye for travel in the area that you are visiting, you will learn what kinds of brush to avoid.

DESERT, ICE FIELDS, AND OTHER WIDE-OPEN SPACES

Navigating in featureless terrain requires maintaining your heading and keeping track of the distance you are covering. There may not be a trail for many miles. While it is possible to navigate with just the sun and stars, you can almost eliminate the guesswork by using a compass and/or GPS to maintain your heading.

Today, most folks who travel across open spaces for extended periods use a handheld GPS to give them their location, pace, and the distance to their destination. If you are using a map and compass, take the time to determine exactly what bearing you will follow across the flats to the next recognizable land feature. In some areas, you could travel for days on one bearing. Carefully keeping track of your pace and the distance traveled will relieve anxiety, particularly if you are on a tight schedule.

TRAVELING AT NIGHT

There are a number of extra risks to consider before traveling in the backcountry at night. Not only is it hard to see land features to orient yourself, but it is often hard to see where you are stepping and can be difficult to read a map. The potential for accidental falls, surprise animal encounters, and becoming woefully lost increases dramatically at night. You will move considerably slower, and your pace may shorten.

In the steep terrain of the canyons or mountains, the potential for walking directly off a small cliff is real. The faster you are moving, the greater the hazard.

If you combine all of the above with sleep deprivation, you are in for quite a challenge. Plan your night navigation very carefully, or expect reluctant sleep in an unplanned spot.

When planning a nighttime route, choose the path that will be the easiest to follow, even if it is a bit longer. Handrails, backstops, and compass readings become critical. Changes in the slope angle that you are walking on may be the only indication of a hill you would have seen clearly from a distance in the daylight. You may need to count your paces, particularly for off-trail travel.

Keeping the above in mind, plan a short on-trail route in an area that you are familiar with the first time you go hiking at night. A nearby city or state park (one where crime is not a major concern) will work. Make it an adventure, and take a few friends with you. Stick together. Don't consider longer distances or unfamiliar areas until you get comfortable with moving in the forest at night. When you do move on to traveling in unfamiliar backcountry areas at night, be sure to write a travel plan, and bring essential gear.

Other Tips for Following Routes

PACE SETTING

The pace you set for your group will depend entirely on your group's goals for the day. Are you out to snap some photos, enjoy the scenery, and have a picnic in a remote place? Or do you have to reach a specific campsite by nightfall? Do you have the entire day to cover several miles of easy hiking? Or are you in the middle of an adventure race? Everyone in the group should agree in advance on what the goal for the day is. Set a pace that suits the goal.

For those times when you do need to move in a hurry, pay careful attention to stopping for breaks. Determine how many breaks you need; more than one every hour may be excessive. Can you eat and drink while you are moving? When you stop, make sure someone keeps an eye on the time. A lot can be accomplished in a 10-minute break: You can change layers, refill water, grab food, and tape that "hot spot" on your heel. Make sure that items that you will need on the trail are accessible and not buried in your pack.

The person in the front should set a pace that is sustainable for the whole group, given the terrain and length of time that you will be traveling. The pace-setter's job is to check in with the other members of the group to make sure the pace is working for everyone. If someone is struggling to keep up, don't let them drift to the back. Put slower hikers in the middle or front so that the group can adjust to a pace that is manageable for everyone.

PACE COUNTING

Estimating your speed and then keeping an eye on your watch is by far the easiest way to gauge distance; it is also the least precise. Over longer distances, and in times when precision is less important, use your hiking speed to estimate distance. To be accurate, you will need to know your speed with and without a pack, on and off the trail, in brush and in the open.

A more precise way to measure distance is by pace counting. During an 8-mile hiking day, pace counting the whole distance is impractical, but if you become interested in orienteering (see chapter 10), you will need to pace count at times.

Figuring out the length of your average pace is simple (see exercise 3 at the end of this chapter). Once you know your average length, you simply need to keep track of your paces. There are a number of ways to do this. Some people use beads on a string or pebbles moved from one hand to another or dropped in a pocket every 100 paces. Find a system that works for you and apply it consistently as you travel.

CONTOURING AND SIDEHILLING

Losing elevation only to regain it later can be a frustrating drain on your group's energy. Two techniques that can be helpful in dealing with this are contouring and sidehilling. Contouring is maintaining the same elevation as you travel, as if you were walking along a contour line on a map. Often, steep terrain can be avoided this way.

Sidehilling is contouring off-trail on a steep slope. When you are sidehilling, each step with your uphill leg will be shorter than each step with your downhill leg. This means that your uphill leg is supporting your entire weight most of the time. If the hill is not very steep, or the distance is not great, sidehilling is not a problem. If you are sidehilling in steep terrain for more than a quarter mile, your uphill leg muscles may begin to complain. Extended sidehilling should be avoided. It is often easier to do an ascending traverse to the ridge above or descend to the base and parallel the hill.

CHECKING THE MAP

Your speed, experience, and memory all play into how often you should be looking at your map. Unless you are racing, you have nothing to lose by taking the time to stop and make sure you are on the right track. While you are practicing the exercises in this book, look at your map at least every five minutes, unless you are cruising alongside a major river or trail with no junctions. Many navigators study their map in detail the night before a long or tricky route to try to memorize as much of the route as they can. This allows them to spend less time looking at the map while they are moving. If visibility becomes a problem (nightfall, bad weather, etc.), the map should be checked even more than usual.

Orient your map every time you stop to look at it. Some navigators keep their map oriented by turning it in their hands as they change directions. At the very least, try to keep your thumb on your location on the map as you travel. By using this technique, known as thumbing, you always know your approximate location on the map and don't have to relocate yourself each time you do a map check. You are also more likely to catch a wrong turn.

STAYING FLEXIBLE

Be flexible. Your maps can only tell you so much. You may have to adjust your plans according to the weather and new information that you discover on the ground. Visualize your route in stages.

If you are unsure where to go, be willing to stop and scout before moving ahead. Seek higher ground for a better view if you need to. Scout in pairs with maps, then regroup to share the scouts' findings.

Exercises

Exercise 1: Getting Off-Trail

Plan and follow your own off-trail route. Take some time to study the map and visualize what the terrain will look like. What are the contour lines telling you about the shape of the terrain? Where are the hills and valleys? How far apart are they? Where will your field of view be blocked by hills in the foreground?

Plan your route. Where will your attack point be? Are there any handrails or backstops you can use? Will the route be out and back, a loop, or a "lollipop" shape?

When you arrive at the trailhead, think of how well what you see matches what you visualized. Does it look the way that you expected it to?

Exercise 2: Staying Oriented

Plan another short hike (2 to 5 miles) that travels mostly off-trail and forms a circle or loop. Keep your map out the whole time you are hiking, with your thumb on your location. Try to keep the map oriented so that north on the map is always pointing toward true north. Can you do it without looking at your compass?

Exercise 3: Learning Your Average Speed

There are two methods that you can use to determine your average speed. The first is to measure your speed in various settings. Take a few minutes to study the chart of average mile times below.

Measure your personal average times and fill in the chart. Obviously, the steepness of the terrain will affect your time. The times above are for a slope between 5 and 10 degrees. If you are in a flatter area, take your time on a hill a quarter- or half-mile long and multiply. Be honest with yourself about your average times, as they will be used to help you estimate your speed in different situations. Take note of the conditions for each speed that you measure. What are your average times at night? How about with a heavy backpack?

AVERAGE SPEED CHART

Time in minutes per mile for an average person with no pack weight

	Road	Trail	Off-Trail	
			Open Woods	Thick Brush
Walking				
Uphill	18	20	22	25+
Flat	15	16	18	20+
Running				
Uphill	11	12	13	N/A
Flat	9	10	11	N/A

You could also set up a pace meter. Go to a track with a quarter-mile lap. Walk the distance with your pack on, counting every time your right foot hits the ground—it takes two steps to make one pace. How many paces does it take you to get around the track? Multiply that number by 4 to get a rough idea of how

AVERAGE SPEED CHART

Time in minutes per mile

	Road	Trail	Off-Trail	
			Open Woods	Thick Brush
Walking				
Uphill				
Flat				
Running				
Uphill				
Flat				

many paces it takes you to walk a mile. Divide 5,280 by that number to get your average pace length in feet.

You can use a similar method on a football or soccer field. Count the number of paces it takes you to walk the field, and divide that number by 100 to get the length of your pace in yards (American football field) or meters (soccer field). Use the following values to convert between metric and English measurements:

1 kilometer = 1,000 meters = 3,281 feet = 1,094 yards

1 mile = 5,280 feet = 1,760 yards = 1,609 meters = 1.609 kilometers

How do you think your pace length will change at night? How about going up or down a steep hill? Put your predictions to the test in the field, and record the results for future route-planning.

| **ALTIMETERS**

What Is an Altimeter (and Do I Need One?)

An altimeter does one thing: It estimates altitude. It is just one more tool to combine with solid map-reading skills for accurate orientation and navigation. If you will be traveling in terrain that is relatively flat (less than 500 feet of elevation change in a travel day), you may not need an altimeter.

If you are navigating in mountainous terrain, knowing your elevation and tracking your elevation changes can be both fun and enlightening. Keeping track of your elevation and location on the map with an altimeter is one way to become familiar with the amount of time and energy it takes to climb or descend in steep terrain. Estimating in advance how long it will take to reach a certain elevation, then checking your actual elevation with an altimeter, can help you understand your group's abilities and limits. Over time, your estimations will become more accurate, and you will become a better navigator.

Two types of altimeters are routinely used for land navigation—barometric altimeters and GPS-based altimeters. Barometric altimeters tend to be slightly more expensive but are also more reliable because their mechanism is simpler than GPS altimeters'. Altimeter functions have become more common in GPS receivers and are plenty accurate for most wilderness navigators.

Barometric Altimeters

Barometers are instruments that measure atmospheric pressure, which is essentially the weight of air above that point. The weight of air is directly related to how much of it is above the instrument: As you ascend to a higher altitude, there is less air above you, which weighs less. As altitude increases, air pressure decreases proportionally. A barometer can register and report the details of this change.

Altimeters are specialized barometers configured to give air pressure measurements in terms of height above sea level. This means that on the summit of Mount Everest, the air pressure will always be much lower than anywhere at sea level. Atmospheric pressure varies with weather patterns, so a barometric altimeter must occasionally be recalibrated when the elevation is known via other means—such as knowing exactly where you are on the map. Suppose you are standing at the summit of Gannett Peak; the height at that point is marked on your map, about 13,800 feet. You can now calibrate your altimeter such that it reads this figure.

Typical digital altimeter

Barometric altimeters are either digital or analog. Over the last decade, digital barometric altimeters have made their way into handheld GPS units and many watches. Note that there is an important difference between a GPS device that derives its altitude using GPS signals and one that measures its altitude using a separate barometric sensor.

Barometric altimeters are surprisingly accurate when used properly. When an altimeter is an integral feature of your watch or GPS, it may be harder to use than a standalone version. Most altimeter watches also display the temperature and your rate of ascent or descent. Some feature alarms that can be set to go off at a certain elevation and log books that automatically record your altitude changes for review later.

DIGITAL BAROMETER/ALTIMETER

There are two distinct disadvantages to using digital altimeters: They are more affected by extreme temperatures, and there is a risk of the battery dying. Most models are inoperable below -5°F (-20°C) or above 120°F (50°C), but this temperature limitation will probably not affect an altimeter watch as long as it stays on your wrist. (If the temperature of your wrist is below -5°F or above 120°F, you have bigger problems than figuring out your elevation.) If you need to take your watch off in extreme temperatures, keep it in an inside pocket. Most models retain altitude information even if the LCD screen goes blank in cold temperatures. For longer expeditions, make sure to change your altimeter's battery before you go, or take a spare and know how to change it. Be wary of models that ask you not to change the battery yourself.

ANALOG BAROMETER/ALTIMETER

Analog altimeters have faded from use for land navigation by all but a handful of high-altitude mountaineers, scientists, and polar explorers. Still, they work well at subfreezing temperatures, have fewer parts to break or malfunction, and are easy to use. They resemble and are carried like a pocket watch. If you're looking to stay below 16,000 feet, there are several analog models under $100. Otherwise, digital may be the way to go. To read an analog altimeter, give it a couple of light taps to loosen the needle, then look straight down on it rather than at an angle.

Considerations for Using Barometric Altimeters

As the weather changes, the air pressure changes, which can throw off your altimeter. Say that you are at camp all day and a low-pressure system moves into your area, causing your altimeter to read several hundred feet higher by the end of the day. One way to overcome this problem is to reset your reference altitude. When you are at a known elevation, like a trail intersection, summit, or lake, double-check your altimeter's reading and adjust it to match the altitude you have for your location on the map. In periods of stable weather, you may not need to reset for several days. Of course, getting a good reading will be most important in bad weather, when visibility is low. Take the time to check the accuracy of your altitude and reset each night in camp, when elevation details are critical.

The designers of digital altimeters have tried several ways to lessen the effects of changing weather readings. Some models allow you to turn off the altimeter while you are in camp. This allows the watch to register the air pressure changes on the barometer, but not on the altimeter. This works well as long as you remember to turn it off each night and turn it back on before leaving camp. Some altimeters have integrated GPS units that can distinguish between changes in elevation (location) and changes in weather, limiting the need to reset. If your altimeter doesn't talk directly to a GPS, expect to either turn off the altimeter or reset it at least once daily in the mountains.

The temperature may also have an adverse effect on your altimeter reading. As the temperature rises and falls, the altimeter's sensor expands and contracts, leading to inaccuracies.

The good news is that most altimeters made within the last decade have a temperature compensation feature that works well when you are not changing elevation. When you are changing elevation and the temperature swings rapidly, there can still be minor problems with temperature-compensated models. As previously mentioned, keeping the altimeter on your wrist or inside your layers while you are moving helps it to stay at a fairly even temperature. Body heat is enough to counter the effects of temperature change in all but very extreme situations.

GPS-Based Altimeters

GPS receivers calculate their position by using signals from reference satellites. The accuracy of their position fix depends on how many satellites they can incorporate into the calculation and the strength of the signals from those satellites. With three satellites acquired, a GPS can produce a 2-D fix. This fix assumes the Earth to be an idealized, perfectly smooth, regular spheroid (i.e., all points on Earth are at altitude zero). By adding more satellites to the calculation (four is the minimum), a GPS receiver can calculate a 3-D fix that can delete the spheroid assumption. This 3-D fix includes altitude information.

Orienting Yourself with an Altimeter

Knowing your elevation can play a part in determining your location. With an accurate reading of your altitude, you can treat a contour line as a line of position. This method is most helpful in steep areas, where elevation changes rapidly as you move. On flat terrain, altitude is less suited to this method.

Some altimeters are more accurate than others. Let's say yours is ±40 feet, which happens to also be the contour interval on your topographic map. The more tightly spaced the contour lines (steep terrain), the narrower the band of terrain where you must be. The more spread out the contour lines (flat terrain), the broader the band of uncertainty.

In reality, a good altimeter is more precise than ±40 feet, but the concept is the same. The more mountainous the terrain, the more certain you can be of your location. In rolling hills or flat terrain, where the elevation is more consistent, an altimeter will be less useful for position-finding.

If you are on a line feature, such as a ridge, trail, or drainage, you may be able to locate yourself on the map by finding where the contour line at your elevation intersects the line feature you are following. This is the same concept as fixing your location with two lines of position. In this case, one of those lines comes from altitude rather than from a river, trail, compass bearing, etc.

Suppose you know your altitude is 9,200 feet, and you also know that you are standing on the Sheep Creek Trail. The intersection of these two lines—the trail and the 9,200 contour line—indicates your location. An important assumption here is that the trail's elevation profile is such that it only crosses 9,200 once. If the trail undulates between 9,000 and 9,500, for example, this method is less useful.

In areas with few land features or low visibility (such as a dense forest), altitude information may be the only way to locate yourself accurately.

Exercise

TRACKING ELEVATION CHANGES

While in the backcountry, check your altitude at campsites, lakes, trail intersections, and other known elevations for several days in a row. How often do you need to reset your reference altitude? How accurate is it? Record any differences in your altimeter reading and known elevation several times each day. Can you determine a typical margin of error for your altimeter? Are the weather changes you see consistent with the changes in the barometer?

COORDINATE SYSTEMS

Imagine that you are an emergency dispatcher for a search-and-rescue team with a rescue helicopter in the northwestern United States. A call comes in about a serious accident on a wilderness trip. The caller is using a satellite phone without GPS or other locator technology. Someone has fallen and needs immediate medical attention. Your job is to determine the exact location of the injured person so that you can dispatch a rescue helicopter. Time is critical.

Them: We've had an accident about five miles north of Badger Lake. My friend hurt his leg and is bleeding all over the place! We need a helicopter!

You: Are you calling from Oregon or Washington?

Them: Oregon. Near Mount Hood.

You: Do you know your numerical coordinates?

Them: Well, no. But I know where we are on the map.

You: Can you tell me what map you are using?

Them: It's the "Green Trails" map of Mount Hood, Oregon, #462.

You: Are you within a mile of any distinct land feature that is named on the map?

Them: We're about two miles from Trail 650, but it turns into Trail 480 farther down.

You: Which direction is Trail 650 from where you are?

Them: Kind of southwest, but really more west than south, I guess.

You: What is the distance and direction of Mount Hood from your current location?

Them: It's on the other map. I'll have to grab it out of the tent. Hold on a minute. [Several minutes pass.] Okay, it's about eight miles west of here.

You: You are eight miles east of Mount Hood, five miles north of Badger Lake, and two miles east-northeast of Trail 650. Is that right?

Them: That sounds right, but, gosh, I'm sorry—I meant to say south of Badger Lake. Can you guys hurry up? My buddy has lost a lot of blood and really needs help fast!

Coordinates take the guesswork out of describing locations. Rather than using land features and triangulation to describe an area, coordinates pinpoint a precise location. By carefully locating a point within a grid on a map, navigators can reference a location on land or sea, without relying on landmarks. If you plan to use GPS, or if there is a chance you may need to give someone your location in an emergency, you should learn how to read and plot coordinates.

Types of Coordinate Systems

A coordinate system is a numbered grid or series of grids laid over a map. By using measurable values on the grid, you can describe an exact location. Most coordinate systems are based on an X axis (horizontal value) and a Y axis (vertical value). Road maps and atlases often use letters for one axis and numbers for another. With a checkerboard-style grid drawn over the map, coordinates such as "7C" give you a more specific area in

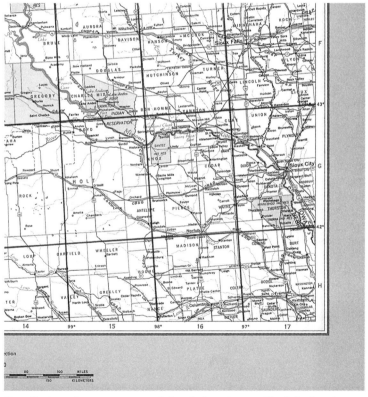

Coordinate systems are an essential part of most maps. The letter/number system shown here in this map of Nebraska and South Dakota is a common method.

which to search for the town or intersection that you are trying to locate.

While there are a number of coordinate systems, the most commonly used for wilderness navigation are the latitude/longitude system and the Universal Transverse Mercator (UTM) system. Generally, land-based navigators using topographic maps favor UTM coordinates. Mariners typically keep with the tradition of using latitude/longitude for describing locations at sea. Most topographic maps are printed with coordinates from at least one system in the margin. All USGS quads feature both types of coordinates. Nautical charts do not include UTM, only latitude/longitude.

Plotting coordinates on a paper map is easier with transparent map rulers that have minutes and seconds marked on them. Make sure that the rulers you're using match the map scale. Some compasses have a map ruler built into the base plate. The rulers you need for latitude/longitude measurements differ from UTM grid readers. Some map tools feature both.

LATITUDE AND LONGITUDE

The latitude/longitude system was the first widely used coordinate system. Created by the ancient scholar Ptolemy around 2,000 years ago, latitude/longitude coordinates are still used by pilots, sailors, land management agencies, and many GPS users. While they are slightly more cumbersome to use than UTM coordinates, you should know latitude/longitude because the people with whom you would communicate in an emergency situation may not know UTM. In general, you should be fluent in the system that is used on the map/chart that you are using.

The latitude/longitude coordinate system is an unprojected grid system, meaning it is independent of whatever projection might be used to render a map. It lays out its grid relative to the spherical Earth, rather than relative to the boundaries of a derived map. Latitude and longitude are used to indicate a physical location on Earth with two numbers. Their measurements are essentially angles, which means these numbers are expressed in degrees, minutes, and seconds. While these may sound like time measurements, they're not.

The latitude/longitude system divides the Earth into 360 degrees of arc. Each degree is subdivided into 60 minutes of arc, and each minute is further divided into 60 seconds. This notation is called DMS (Degree, Minute, Second). An angle of 20 degrees, 42 minutes, and 30 seconds will be expressed as 20°42'30". The minutes/seconds system is falling out of common use for most map users, and some navigators are opting to measure in degrees and decimal minutes. As there are 60 seconds to a minute, the 20°42'30" from the above example would be expressed as 20°42.5' when using decimal minutes.

Historical Note

The DMS is a sexagesimal (base-60) counting system that was invented by the ancient Sumerians. Sumerian geometry laid the foundation for classic Greek geometry and mathematics.

Describing a Point Using Latitude and Longitude

Latitude represents a north–south position on Earth. The equator is at latitude zero. As you move north, latitude increases to 90 degrees at the North Pole. The southern hemisphere operates in the same way: The South Pole is at 90 degrees south. Lines of latitude are parallel to one another and evenly spaced (they are sometimes called parallels). Lander, Wyoming, is approximately 43 degrees north of the equator, so its latitude is in the neighborhood of N43°. Its actual latitude is N42° 49.98''. Northern latitudes are often expressed as positive numbers, and southern latitudes are often expressed as negative numbers. So, the North Pole is simply 90°, the South Pole is -90°, and Lander is 42° 49.98'.

Longitude represents an east–west position on Earth. Lines of longitude are called meridians. With latitude, there is a natural reference for zero (the equator). There is not an obvious starting point for zero longitude, however. The starting point, or reference where longitude is zero, was adopted by an international convention called the International Meridian Conference, which took place in Washington, DC, in 1884. It is called the prime meridian. All meridians converge at the poles, which means that the surface distance between two degrees of longitude is different at each latitude. If you look at a globe with latitude and longitude marked, you'll see that the longitude lines are much closer together near the poles than on the equator. This makes measuring longitude a bit trickier than measuring latitude. Lander is west of the reference meridian by about 108 degrees. The longitude for Lander is W108° 43.84'.

The 1:24,000-scale maps have a height of 7.5 minutes of latitude and a width of 7.5 minutes of longitude, and they

Lines of longitude (left) and latitude (right)

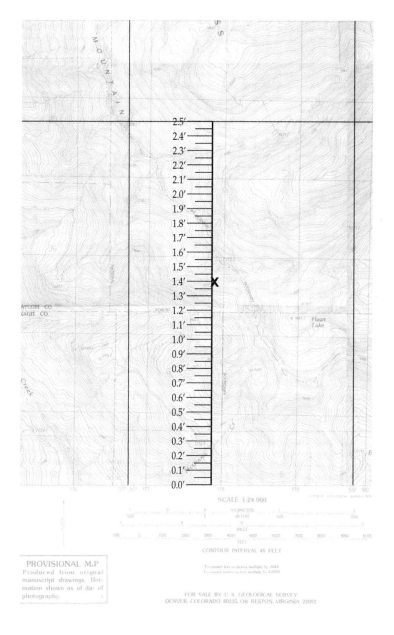

The X lies 1.4 minutes north of the 48° 37'30" line on the Twin Sisters map, giving it a latitude of 48° 38.9' north.

are called 7.5-minute series maps. If you look at a 7.5-minute USGS map, you'll see measurements of latitude and longitude in the margins at 2.5-minute intervals. Measurements of latitude appear as black ticks in the left and right margins, and measurements of longitude appear on the top and the bottom. Within the frame of the map, four small black crosses appear where the lines of latitude and longitude intersect. They look like the tiny crosshairs you would see through a rifle scope. These marks make drawing in latitude and longitude lines easy.

Determining Latitude of a Known Point on the Map

To determine latitude from a known point, orient a map ruler vertically (north to south) so that it spans the lines of latitude that the point falls between. When you're in the northern hemisphere, the zero-minute end of the ruler should be on the southern line of latitude. Read the value from the ruler at the given point, and add it to the latitude at the zero end of the ruler. In the illustration on page 119, X is at the 1.4' mark. The 0.0 mark on the ruler is at 48° 37' 30" or 48° 37.5'. Adding 1.4' to 48° 37.5' gives a resulting latitude of 48 degrees, 38.9 minutes north.

Determining Longitude of a Known Point on the Map

To measure longitude, hold the map ruler diagonally. Place it so that it spans the lines of longitude, with the point to be measured between the lines. The zero end of the ruler should be touching one meridian, and the 2.5' line should be touching the other meridian. (Remember, there are 2.5 minutes between meridians on the USGS quad.) You may need to extend the longitude lines above or below the map to properly position the ruler. Slide the ruler vertically toward the point, keeping each end on a line of longitude. Keep sliding until the edge of the ruler touches the point to be measured. If you can't get the ruler in the right position, try rotating it 90 degrees to switch

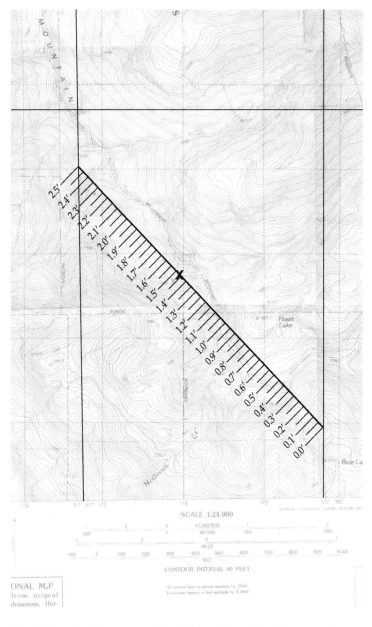

SCALE 1:24 000

CONTOUR INTERVAL 40 FEET

The X lies 1.47 minutes west of the 121° 55' line, giving it an approximate longitude of 121° 56.47' west.

the ends. In the example, X is at 1.47' on the map ruler. Adding 1.47' to 121° 55' gives a resulting longitude of 121 degrees, 56.47 minutes west.

Plotting a Point on the Map from Latitude and Longitude

To plot the location of given coordinates, first find the latitude by measuring up from the southern grid line and making a small line on the map that is parallel to the other lines of latitude. Then, plot the longitude coordinate. The best way to do this is to put your map ruler between two of the map's meridians, make a small tick at the correct longitude, then move the ruler vertically and make another tick. Connecting the two ticks should give you a line that lies along the given line of longitude, at the correct angle. Double-check your marks, then extend those lines using a straightedge and a light pencil. The point is where the plotted lines of latitude and longitude intersect.

UTM COORDINATES

The Mercator projection, named after a sixteenth-century Flemish inventor, was created for sailors to determine their course. There are a few different kinds of Mercator projections; the transverse Mercator is good for general-purpose maps below a certain scale.

Because the UTM system is based on uniform grids of 1,000 square meters, it is considerably easier to use than latitude and longitude, which require you to use two different rulers or turn your ruler diagonally. UTM is to coordinate systems what the metric system is to measurements of distance—in fact, all measurements are in units of 10.

The UTM grid system divides the earth into zones. Sixty primary zones run north to south, and twenty optional zones run east to west. The primary zones are represented by numbers, while the optional zones are represented by letters. Austin, Texas, for example, is in zone 14R. The letter *R* indicates that the UTM coordinate given is located in the northern hemisphere. (Often the letter is left off the zone description because it is not necessary.) Take a look at your map. USGS maps list the zone in the text at the bottom left corner of the margin. You should always include the zone with the UTM coordinates when giving your location. Which zone are you in right now?

Each zone is further divided into numbered grids. The characteristics of the transverse Mercator projection at this scale are such that we can effectively treat lines as square and straight. Each of these UTM grids is 1 kilometer square. The designation is expressed in units of meters, with a particular point on the grid specified as the number of meters east and north in that zone—these are called the "easting" and "northing" values. The full-length version of these values is located at the top left and bottom right borders of each USGS quad. Take a moment now to locate them on your map. They follow this format: 442000mE, 3665000mN. The digits that represent thousands of meters, and tens of thousands of meters, are enlarged to help you quickly locate which kilometer reference lines to use.

Although some newer USGS quads come with printed UTM grid lines, most do not. In order to more accurately plot coordinates, you can draw these lines on your map. UTM tick marks are printed in blue along the border, and usually have a corresponding number in black next to each tick. A 24-inch ruler can be used to draw grid lines connecting these ticks. To draw lines in the field, you can fold the edge of the map over and use the map itself as an impromptu straightedge.

Map ruler
(not to scale)

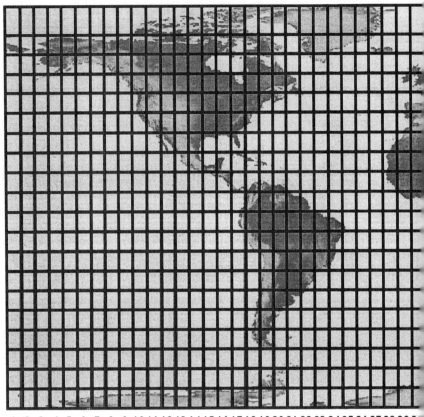

The Universal Transverse Mercator system is a coordinate system that divides the surface of the Earth into a series of smaller regions.

In order to read and plot UTM coordinates, you must have a UTM grid reader that matches the scale of the map (1:24,000 for USGS quads). In a pinch, grid readers can be made in the field by transferring the 100-meter marks from the map's metric distance scale to the upper right corner of a straight-edged piece of paper.

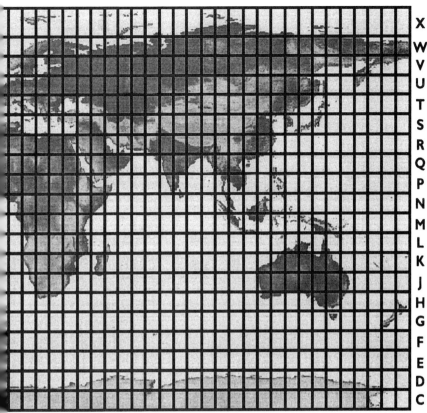

32 33 34 35 36 37 38 39 40 41 42 43 44 45 46 47 48 49 50 51 52 53 54 55 56 57 58 59 60

Determining UTM Coordinates from a Point on the Map

To read the UTM coordinates for a known point X on the map, place the grid reader directly over the grid where the X is located. Read the easting value first. Start from the closest vertical grid line to the left (west) of the X; in the diagram on page 126, this is 581000mE. To get the easting coordinate for the X, add the number of 100-meter squares you count to X from the vertical grid line. In this case, the number of squares is two, so the easting value is 581200mE. You read the northing value by counting up from the lower (southern) horizontal grid

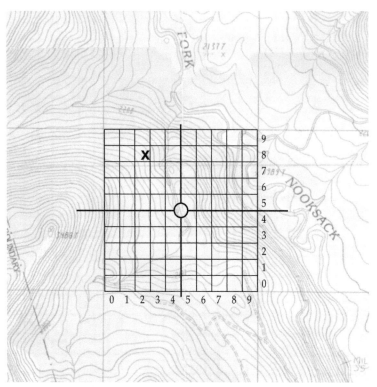

A UTM reader lines up with grid lines on a topo map and allows you to reference an exact location in the UTM system. In this example from the USGS quad for Twin Sisters Mountain in Washington State, the coordinates of the X within the UTM grid are approximately 200mE, 800mN. (The full coordinates are 581200mE, 5390800mN.)

line. Here, the northing value for X is 5390800mN. The easting and northing values give you your location to the nearest 100 meters, plus or minus 50 meters (half a soccer field).

To be more precise, you can read to 10-meter increments. Imagine ten tick marks along the bottom of the 100-meter square surrounding X. The center of X is about seven ticks to the right of the "2" line. The precise easting value is therefore 581270mE.

Plotting a Point on the Map from UTM Coordinates

To plot a point on the map from given coordinates, reverse the process for reading. Place the grid reader on the right of the corresponding vertical grid line. Then, keeping the reader on that grid line, move it vertically up or down the map until it is on the correct horizontal grid line. Count the correct number of 100-meter squares in from both gridlines and, looking through the grid reader, visualize the point you wish to mark on the map. Then move the grid reader and mark the X. Lastly, reposition the grid reader and double-check your mark.

TOWNSHIP AND RANGE LINES

This grid system was employed in the United States primarily for making cadastral maps (maps describing land ownership). Some USGS maps still feature red grid lines that depict the US Public Land Survey, which employed this grid system. These lines divide land into square-mile sections, but rarely run from true north to south.

Township and range grids are still used in land ownership documents and land management designations in the western United States. You may see them marked on older USGS topographic maps. Do not confuse them with other grid lines, and do not use them for compass work. The township and range lines are a system used only in the United States.

Converting Coordinates

If you find yourself needing to convert coordinates from UTM to latitude/longitude, or vice versa, there are several easy solutions. The first is to use a GPS receiver—see chapter 8 for a detailed explanation. Another is to use an online conversion website.

Exercises

Exercise 1: Determining Coordinates Given a Point on a Map

Mark a point in each quadrant of your map. Using a map ruler and a grid reader, determine the latitude and the longitude as well as the UTM coordinates for each point. Have another person double-check your coordinates by erasing your marks and plotting the coordinates you give them.

Exercise 2: Determining Coordinates without Map Tools

Once you have had some practice with grid readers and map rulers, test your ability to estimate a position on the map. In non-emergency situations, where accuracy is less critical, you may choose to "eyeball" coordinates and work without map tools. Pick a couple of spots on your map, and try to determine coordinates for those locations by sight. After you have written down your eyeball estimates, double-check them using a grid reader or a map ruler. How close were you?

Conclusion

If plotting coordinates seems tedious, that's because it is at first. But after a few successful attempts, it can become routine. While knowing how to manually plot coordinates is an important skill to have, digital map software and GPS are making the process of plotting coordinates on paper maps much less common. But watch out! Murphy's Law dictates that the one time you really need to call in your coordinates in an emergency situation, your GPS will have just used up the last of your batteries.

GPS

If you can think of your compass as a bicycle for a moment, a handheld GPS is more like a motorcycle. It can take you a long distance with less effort, but it has more parts that can break down—and it runs out of power after being used for a while. It's also quite a bit more expensive, and it comes with a bigger owner's manual. Just as on a motorcycle you don't get the same sort of exercise that you do on a bicycle, the muscle between your ears will get less of a workout if you navigate exclusively by GPS. Here's the big question: If you were going on a long motorcycle trip and could carry your bicycle in your pocket, would you?

Today, it is still imprudent to head days-deep into the backcountry without a map and compass—GPS or not. Electronic things, just like motorized things, can and do break. A GPS or smartphone is not a replacement for good map skills and good judgment. Learn how to read a topographic map and use a compass before relying on electronics to tell you where to go. Over the last decade, search-and-rescue stories have been adding up of GPS users who didn't have adequate navigation skills or weren't carrying a topo map. If you really want to become a competent land navigator, use your map and compass to navigate, and only use your GPS to track, mark a waypoint, or when traveling in low visibility situations. Whether you have a GPS receiver or not, learn to read the terrain, and always bring along a map and compass.

What Is GPS?

Global Positioning System (GPS) is the common name for a comprehensive system of satellites, ground control stations, and the handheld device that displays position information for users in the field. It is but one of several Global Navigation Satellite Systems (GNSS) currently deployed or in development. GLONASS, for example, is the Russian constellation of satellites that does essentially the same thing as the US-launched GPS. "Galileo" is the European Union version.

For most folks, GPS refers to the electronic device in their hands that tells them their position, regardless of which satellites are in use. This is the GPS receiver—the small gadget that can interpret the radio signals from satellites and determine your location. Most modern smartphones have GPS capabilities built in. Many newer handheld receivers use both the US and Russian satellites, improving the speed and accuracy of fixing location.

At its core, a GPS reports location information only: latitude and longitude (although it can be configured to report position using many different grid systems). Early models of consumer handhelds did only this, and it was then up to the user to plot that location on a map or chart to get a graphic context for the location. These days, a GPS that did only this would not be commercially viable. GPS handhelds (and GPS-enabled smartphones) use location information to provide much more information:

- Your location displayed in context on a digital map or chart.
- Your recent travel speed (by comparing successive locations, the unit can compute how fast you have been moving—average, maximum, and current).
- Your distance traveled.

- The distance to a destination.
- Your estimated time of arrival at a known destination.
- Your current heading or direction of travel (much like how it computes speed, the handheld can compute the direction you are traveling by comparing successive locations along your recent travel path).
- The bearing to a destination.
- Internet-enabled GPS devices, such as smartphones, can also display the locations, bearings, and travel times to nearby points of interest.

All of these features are functions of the handset, not the GPS satellite system.

A Brief History of GPS

In the early 1970s, the US Department of Defense launched the first GPS satellites. Initially, their primary use was for weapons-system targeting. The US military coordinated satellite launches and eventually planned the satellite constellation known as NAVSTAR (Navigation Satellite Timing and Ranging). With each new satellite, the signals became more consistent and accurate. By 1994, twenty-four satellites were in place, and NAVSTAR became fully operational.

Today, the NAVSTAR satellites orbit the Earth on one of six different paths. At about 12,500 miles above Earth, they move at 7,000 miles per hour, completing a full orbit every twelve hours. On clear nights, outside of population centers, they are easily visible with the naked eye. The current satellites are replaced about every ten years. They are solar powered and consist of a computer, a radio transmitter, and an atomic clock. Government-monitored ground stations track them and keep them in their proper orbits.

GPS receivers need to be able to track the signal from at least four satellites at one time in order to fix position accurately. They determine position by measuring their distance from each satellite. The means of determining distance is based on a shared time standard. Through a complex time exchange protocol, all GPS receivers and satellites agree on the precise time with exceptional accuracy. To achieve the required precision, the clocks from the GPS satellites must agree to an accuracy of under 20 nanoseconds. That is a tiny time slice—light travels only about 6 meters in that time. A GPS receiver can calculate the time it takes for a radio transmission to travel from a satellite, and from that time deduce its exact distance from that satellite.

With knowledge of the distance from, and positions of, four or more GPS satellites, a receiver can calculate its own position. This system relies upon the receiver doing the majority of the computational work. The GPS satellites do little more than "ping" their own location and the exact time.

At the time that commercial GPS units came onto the market, the Department of Defense was concerned about the high level of accuracy of this new technology, which was becoming widely available. The government introduced "Selective Availability" (SA) in order to degrade the accuracy of these civilian units—SA purposefully adds errors into NAVSTAR data to reduce accuracy to about 300 feet. On May 2, 2000, Selective Availability was turned off in the United States. The accuracy of civilian GPS units went from 300 feet to less than 50 feet. Even more accurate is the Wide Area Augmentation System (WAAS), a Federal Aviation Administration system that combines data from ground stations with satellite data to increase GPS accuracy. WAAS-activated GPS receivers are accurate to within 10 feet. (On the downside, they are more expensive and use more batteries.) These advances in accuracy coincided with a boom in GPS sales and applications.

In sensitive areas, the US Department of Defense may jam GPS signals to prevent others from using commercial receivers. In recent years, controversy has raged over the deployment of the European Union's own GPS satellite system, "Galileo." Galileo is scheduled to become fully operational in 2018. It will have thirty satellites and allow for accuracy to within 3 feet. Obviously, the United States will be less able to selectively degrade signals from this new system.

Depending on the features of the model you have, and how it integrates with map software, there are a number of things that GPS can do for you, including giving you a real-time display of your current location. The GPS system is designed to provide location information, and not much else. The computations for determining location are made within the handset, not in satellites or in NAVSTAR computers. Any other useful applications for that location data are also a function of the features in your handset: map display, computing direction or distance traveled, waypoint management, altitude, proximity alarms—these are all more-or-less standard features of quality GPS units. These features are not universal, and accessing them will involve different interface on each type of GPS.

There are a growing number of handheld and wrist-top GPS units available today. Think of the suggestions provided in this chapter as a supplement to your manufacturer's user manual.

Who Should Buy a GPS?

Asking yourself if you actually need a handheld GPS for backcountry travel is worthwhile. Many folks venture into the wilderness precisely to get away from the digital screens that we tend to spend so much time in front of. Despite what commercials and magazine advertisements tell you, not every backcountry traveler needs a handheld GPS. Whether you should purchase a GPS unit depends on where you will be traveling and for what purpose. It also depends on what other gadgets you have in your toolbox. Many outdoor electronics already have integrated GPS technology: smartphones, two-way radios, cameras, and even ski goggles. GPS units are useful during navigation in featureless terrain such as oceans, desert, and polar regions. They also work wonders in low-visibility conditions, such as when traveling at night or in nasty storms.

Here are a few questions to aid your decision: Will you be traveling for extended periods of time in areas where the terrain is difficult to see? What are the consequences of being disoriented in the areas that you are planning to visit? Will you be sticking to shorter trips into the mountains or canyons? Do new toys excite you, or do they seem like one more thing to lug along or lose? Will you be spending most of your time in the jungle under a dense tree canopy or in another environment where GPS may not work very well? Is it important to know your exact speed and distance traveled? Do you already own a GPS-enabled smartphone, and do you have the ability to recharge it in the field?

Operating a GPS

GETTING THE RIGHT SETTINGS

Before getting started, it is necessary to make sure that you, your map, and your GPS are speaking the same language. Take the time to get your settings correct each time you travel to a new area.

Datum

A key piece of the GPS puzzle is the theoretical model used to represent the shape of the Earth. GPS receivers compute their locations and altitudes based on a mathematical description of the Earth's shape. The Earth is not a perfectly round sphere; it is "squashed" a little bit, making it more of an ellipsoid than a sphere. But even this ellipsoid is not regular and symmetrical. The shape of the Earth is difficult to model well, and one model—called a datum—that matches the Earth's shape for one part of the world may be totally off for another part. There are hundreds of these models made to suit different mapping needs for different places around the world.

What all of this means is that you must always make sure that the datum setting in your GPS matches the datum of your printed map. If your GPS is using a different datum than your map, the GPS coordinates may be hundreds of meters off from your location on the map. On a USGS map, the datum is indicated in the margin at the bottom of the map. Luckily, most topo maps use the World Geodetic System of 1984 Datum (WGS 84), which matches the default datum used in most GPS receivers. Older topographic maps in the United States are based on North American Datum of 1927 (NAD 27). A common mistake is to use a map based on NAD 27 without setting your GPS to that datum. This mismatch in datum can produce errors of up to 800 feet. Many people also forget to change the datum setting when they travel internationally.

Format
Another setting to check is the format used to display coordinates. You can choose UTM, several versions of latitude/longitude, or one of many other options. Unless you are traveling in one of the polar regions, UTM or latitude/longitude will likely suit your needs. On the position format screen, there may be several options for how to view your latitude and longitude. You can choose degrees, minutes, and seconds (D, M, S); degrees and decimal minutes (D, M.M); or decimal degrees (D.DD). Which option you choose is not as important as knowing how to measure it on your map. Pick the display to which your map ruler is calibrated.

Units
Another setting to consider is metric/statute distances. This choice should be based on the system that you are most comfortable with, and which system your map uses. Statute

distances are given in miles, yards, and feet; metric distances are given in kilometers and meters. Generally, it's best to have your GPS set to whatever units are displayed on your map.

If all of this seems a bit complex, relax—you won't need to change your settings every time you go out. Unless you're a jet-setter, you'll probably be using the same map datum most (if not all) of the time.

ACQUIRING SIGNALS

When you turn your GPS on for the first time in a new area, it will take a few minutes to acquire and process satellite signals. This process can take quite a bit longer if the GPS does not have a clear view of the sky.

Once the GPS has acquired several satellite signals, it can compute its position. A GPS needs to simultaneously communicate with at least four satellites to compute a 2-D fix placed on the modeled (i.e., theoretical) surface of the Earth. With additional satellites, the GPS can get a 3-D fix that includes altitude information. Adding satellites increases the precision of the fix.

Your GPS will give you an estimated degree of accuracy as it acquires and loses satellite signals. With current technology and NAVSTAR satellites, recreational GPS receivers are accurate to within about 50 feet (15 meters). Your GPS may claim to be more accurate, but don't bet your life on it. When you add in the human error factor, getting a position report to within 30 feet of your target is actually quite remarkable. Unless you are literally looking for a needle in a haystack, 30 feet should be as close as you need to get to see your objective. A tent, a pond, a trail junction, a car, a bicycle, and even a baseball are visible from 50 feet in most terrain. If you are navigating with your GPS, it is smart to slow down and look for your objective once the GPS says you are within 100 feet.

WAYPOINTS

Waypoints are coordinates that are stored in your GPS for a specific location. Think of a waypoint as a "bookmark" for a place. You can have your GPS mark a waypoint at any time and anywhere that you have a signal. Waypoints can also mark your current location. This can be helpful if you want to return there later or track where you've been on a map.

There may be times when you would like to enter the coordinates for a location that you have never visited and ask the GPS to direct you to that location. This is how the military sends precision "smart bombs" to their targets and how geocachers locate caches. You must first determine the coordinates that you would like to enter. This can be done by plotting them on your topo map or by using Google Earth or offline map software with your GPS connected to your computer. The GPS will automatically remember the waypoint and assign it a generic name (often numerical: 001, 002, etc.). These waypoints can be renamed to prevent confusion: Car, Camp 1, Fishing Spot 4/25/2018, Waterfall, etc. The best names combine something unique about the location with the date or sequence visited.

THE GOTO FUNCTION

Once you have waypoints recorded in the GPS, you can ask it to point you directly to a waypoint by using the "Goto" function. The unit will display an arrow that points directly at the waypoint and tells you your current distance from that waypoint.

Remember that you may still have some route-finding to do. The GPS may be telling you that your waypoint is only 2 miles south of your current location, but it will not tell you that you need to cross a 3,000-foot canyon or that a bridge is out. As always, the most direct route may or may not be the best route.

The display arrow on a GPS does not work like the magnetic needle on your compass. Unless you have a unit with a built-in digital compass, the GPS cannot determine which way it is oriented when it is sitting still. This means that any time you are route-finding with your GPS, you must be walking and looking at the display screen at the same time. Don't trip over that rock!

The advantage to route-finding with a GPS is that it is easy to go around obstacles (like a lake or a boulder field) and get right back on your bearing. The display arrow will adjust to your current location and point directly toward your target. Gone is the need to make 90-degree turns and count steps off your bearing.

On longer treks you can save batteries by using the GPS to get your direction, sighting a landmark with your compass, turning the GPS off, and following the bearing with your compass. Stay on the compass bearing until you have another big obstacle to go around and need to change your heading. Don't set a bearing with the compass right next to the GPS—the metallic parts and batteries in the GPS will throw off the compass needle. When using the compass, keep it at least 6 inches away from the GPS.

TRACKING

Most handheld GPS units feature automatic tracking. This means that you can set the GPS to automatically mark points at intervals according to either distance or time. Use the "pan track" feature to scroll back in time to any location you have visited. Many units also have a "track-back" feature that enables the GPS to direct you back along your tracks. This can be helpful if you are following a difficult route in low visibility; or in an emergency you can ask the GPS to guide you in retracing your steps—think of needing to return to a scarce water source in canyon country, or to base camp when a blizzard hits in the mountains. If you have a computer connection, you can download your tracks onto a digital topographic map and see where you've been.

While using the tracking feature has a number of advantages, if you pass through dense brush while your GPS is tracking, a weak satellite signal may cause it to drop a few of the tracks. Tracking also requires more batteries than occasionally turning the unit on to check your location. If you use tracking, have plenty of extra batteries on hand or the means to recharge.

Choosing the Right GPS

Like other outdoor toys, GPS units are getting smaller, lighter, more specialized, and easier to use. Which one you choose to buy depends largely on how you answer these questions:

What is the main activity you will be doing with GPS?
Some models offer specialized features for cycling, running, hunting, fishing, climbing, or geocaching. For athletes, special software is available for monitoring training. If you are looking for something strictly for alerting the authorities in an emergency, rather than a navigation tool, you might consider purchasing a satellite messenger or personal locator beacon. These have built-in GPS for reporting location to authorities.

Do you own a GPS-enabled smartphone?
If you own a smartphone, you might be better off purchasing an application that enables you to use the phone's GPS hardware. However, using the GPS will drain the phone's battery charge more quickly, so if you plan on using your smartphone on extended wilderness trips, you will need a system for recharging it.

How much can you spend?
Accuracy of about 50 feet is standard for today's recreational-model GPS units. Newer models featuring Wide Area

Augmentation System (WAAS) or Differential GPS capabilities are accurate to within about 10 feet. Unless you are buying a professional-grade GPS unit (for surveying or GIS integration), more money does not necessarily mean better accuracy.

Handheld or wrist-top?
For many people on the move, a wrist-top computer or smart-watch is a good tool for wilderness travel. If your watch tells you the altitude, air temperature, and time, along with your heart rate, speed, and location, it's clearly more than the windup watch that your grandpa wore. There are things to consider when deciding whether to get a wrist-top or a handheld model. If you're planning to do any long-distance running, adventure racing, or fast-packing with your GPS, then size and weight are important, and a wrist-top may be the way to go. If you don't see yourself ever racing, consider a handheld GPS or smart-phone instead—they are generally more user-friendly, with more features and a slightly larger size, which makes it easier to manually enter data. If you want to be able to see a digital map on your GPS, you will need a handheld or smartphone. Also, if you will be entering waypoints in the field, the tiny buttons on wrist-tops can be tedious, although you may be able to enter routes and waypoints into some wrist-tops by uploading them from your computer. Overall, it's important to balance ease of use with the need to save weight.

Do you need computer compatibility?
If you're not a computer person, you might save a few bucks by buying an older GPS that isn't computer-friendly. If you are a computer person, make sure that the software and GPS you buy will work with your computer and operating system. Most of the receivers sold today are designed to interface with a Mac, PC, or both.

Do you need a map display?

While all GPS receivers have some sort of display screen, not all of them can display maps. Many wrist-tops and cheaper handhelds with smaller screens will not display maps. As far as digital map displays go, there are three kinds of GPS units suitable for land navigation:

- Those that display digital maps on the unit
- Those that don't display digital maps on the unit, but may still link up to your computer
- GPS-enabled smartphones or tablets (which typically do feature a map display)

A map display on your GPS may not be worth the extra cost and shorter battery life. Being able to see maps on your GPS screen is pretty cool, but whether you really need it depends in part on what kind of traveling you will be doing. Do you need to go fast and light, or are you setting up a three-week base camp somewhere?

Batteries

If you are depending on electronics for help with navigation, make sure you have enough battery power for your entire trip. For most situations, this means carrying at least one spare set of batteries. Before heading into the backcountry, know how long a set of batteries will last in your GPS.

When your GPS is on and operating normally, it is processing satellite signals about every second. Some handheld models will burn through a set of batteries in three to six hours if the unit is continuously on. Use battery saver mode, or turn the unit off until you need it. Make sure, however, that you practice with it and know how to navigate with it.

GPS and GPS-enabled apps on your phone can do some amazing route-finding in frontcountry environments, where roads, traffic conditions, etc., can be monitored. GPS systems do not (yet) have the ability to route-find in the backcountry. While following the magic GPS arrow can be handy, you may have a tough time getting up the cliffs and through the crevasse fields it is pointing you toward. Your map software won't do route-finding, river crossings, or crevasse rescues for you. Remember that just because the arrow points you toward the most direct route doesn't mean it's the best route, or the safest route. Don't let your smartphone or GPS get you into terrain that you don't have the proper skills to manage.

Exercises

Exercise 1: Plotting Coordinates and Navigating with GPS

Find a topographic map of the area where you live, or an area you know well, and plot the coordinates for a known destination within walking distance. Measure the distance on your map between you and your destination using a string and the map scale. Enter the coordinates into your GPS, and mark the destination as a waypoint.

Use the Goto function on the GPS to direct you toward your destination. What does the GPS give as the total distance? As you approach your waypoint, keep an eye on the direction arrow and estimated distance. On some GPS units, the distance will change from miles to feet (or kilometers to meters) as you get close to your destination.

If you turn out to be off by more than 100 feet, double-check to see that you plotted the point correctly, entered it correctly, and have all of your settings correct in the GPS.

Once you've practiced using your GPS around town several times, begin plotting coordinates and using the GPS to assist in navigating off-trail to more-remote locations with less-visible land features. Try getting a bearing with the GPS and then following the bearing using your map and compass.

For a real challenge, try traveling at night, off-trail, with the GPS. Don't forget to take a partner(s) and some emergency bivouac gear.

Exercise 2: Determining Average Speed

Use your GPS to determine your average speed walking, running, or cycling. How do those averages change over different kinds of terrain (on/off-road, on/off-trail, up/downhill)?

Exercise 3: Finding a Geocache

The website www.geocaching.com describes geocaching as "a real-world outdoor treasure hunting game." Players try to locate hidden containers, called geocaches, using GPS-enabled devices and then share their experiences online. Participating in a cache hunt is a good way to take advantage of the features and capabilities of a GPS unit. The basic idea is to have individuals and organizations set up caches all over the world and share the locations of these caches on the internet. GPS users can then use the location coordinates to find the caches.

A cache is a hidden container, such as an army surplus ammo box, containing a variety of inexpensive trinkets and a registry to keep track of who has found it. If a visitor takes something from the cache, they leave something in its place. While some caches are designed to be found by off-road vehicle users, others are hidden specifically for those on foot. Some caches are obvious, but others are cleverly disguised to blend in with their environment (like a hollow rock).

To give geocaching a try, visit www.geocaching.com. When you select a cache, the coordinates will appear in both UTM and latitude/longitude. Make sure that you have the right map, and that if you're using UTM, the datum given with the coordinates matches the datum on your map.

For an additional challenge to both your plotting and navigation skills, try to locate a geocache without using a GPS. By plotting coordinates manually and using your map-reading skills, this can be accomplished. However, be prepared to spend some time wandering around. If you have a GPS, take it along as a backup in case you aren't having any luck—caches are often cleverly hidden.

A few reminders about geocaching:

- Never search for or place caches in designated wilderness areas.
- Comply with local and federal laws, and don't trespass on private property.
- Bring something to leave in the cache.

Good luck!

LOST

If you are traveling off-trail through wild areas on a regular basis, sooner or later you will get lost. In rolling terrain, thick forest, or weather that limits visibility, even the best navigators can become disoriented. This temporary sort of confusion is normal. Usually, getting to a place with a better view, or orienting the map with a compass, is all that you need to do to relocate yourself and get back on track.

Good navigators have the ability to recognize when they are starting to veer off route and to know when to stop and return to a known location. Making mistakes is part of navigation; refusing to admit them until it's too late, forcing your group to spend an unplanned night in the wilderness, is not. There's no shame in asking others in your group for help.

Nonetheless, at some point you may become truly lost. The difference between being temporarily disoriented and being truly lost is that you aren't truly lost until you've put some effort into locating yourself and failed.

Prevention

People generally get lost in the wild because they become separated from their party, have inadequate navigation skills, or leave the map and compass behind. People who get into real trouble are those who get lost and don't have adequate skills, food, or gear to stay alive until they are found.

BEFORE THE TRIP

A few simple trip-planning steps will make a world of difference. If you've taken the following precautions before leaving, you will be less likely to get lost—and much more at ease if you do get lost.

- Know your navigation techniques. Don't wait until you are 5 miles into the backcountry before learning to read a map and compass. Make sure your navigation skills are always a few notches above where they need to be for the terrain you are in. Practice in city parks or near trailheads before setting out on a multiday trip.
- Carry essential gear and extra food so that you can spend an unplanned night or two out if an emergency arises.
- For overnight trips, write a travel plan, and leave it with a responsible adult. Be sure to include a detailed description of your route and return time.
- Study your route before the trip. Brief your group so that everyone knows what to expect.
- Have more than one navigator in your group. (What happens if the only person who knows how to read a map gets sick or injured?)

STAYING FOUND

Most people who have been lost in the wild say they "had a feeling" they were not heading in the right direction. Why did they continue? Their answers range from "I just wasn't sure, so I kept going" to "I didn't want to have to hike all the way back up that hill." Don't play mind games with yourself by trying to make the terrain fit the map. If you're not sure, it's probably time to stop and ask others in your group for their opinions.

There is a difference between being temporarily uncertain of your location in an area with limited visibility and being disoriented, even when you can clearly see distant land features. Your job as a navigator is to make sure you don't let the first situation become the second one by panicking and plowing off course at high speed. The first thing you must do is stop and consider your options.

Imagine a continuum of certainty about your location and the direction in which you are heading. On one end of the continuum, you are absolutely sure where you are and which way you're facing, like when you are standing in front of your house. On the other end of the continuum, you can't recognize a single land feature, and you doubt you're even on the map. As you start to slip down the continuum, you should be pulling out your compass more frequently to keep track of your direction. If you're somewhere near the middle of the continuum, it is time to turn around and retrace your steps. If you reach the truly lost end, you've likely wandered so far from your route that you might not be able to find it again.

Here are some additional tips for staying found:

- Keep everyone in your group involved in the navigation, even if they are not experts. Relying on a single person to do all of the navigating for a group is usually a mistake.
- When visibility is good, stop and do map checks. Try to take breaks in areas where you have a good view so that you can confirm your location.
- Look for handrails and backstops to help keep you on route.
- Keep the group together. If you have to split up, do it according to a plan, and have a contingency plan if one party doesn't make it back by a set time.
- Don't commit to a route unless you know you will be able to either retrace your footsteps or complete the

route. Never descend when you can't climb back up, or climb when you can't descend, unless you are absolutely sure you want to commit.

- If you'll be following the same path on the return trip, look over your shoulder on the way out to see what it will look like on the way back.
- Have a designated "sweep" person. Their job is to follow along and make sure that no one is drifting too far behind the rest of the group.

But What If I Really Do Get Lost?

Stop! Do not continue! Every step in the wrong direction is a step in the wrong direction. Stand still, pull out your maps, take off your pack, sit, and think. The worst thing you can do is speed ahead.

Most people who are lost have a mental map of where they think they are. But that map is, of course, wrong. This is why lost people who keep moving tend to move quite far in the wrong direction. Initial efforts toward getting found need to focus on finding landmarks to get back onto the map, not moving quickly using an incorrect mental map.

Try not to panic. This can waste valuable energy that could be used to determine your location. Relax—merely being lost is not an emergency. Even if you are injured, out of food, and alone in a blinding snowstorm, giving up, or losing your cool, will not do you or anyone else any good. Your actions, once you realize you are lost, are critical.

Consider retracing your steps. What is the last point at which you knew where you were? How long has it been since you were there? What direction have you been traveling to get to where you are? Can you reverse your course given the daylight you have left?

If there is a clearing or high point nearby where you can get your bearings, consider going there to check your maps. If you have recently become separated from your group, don't be ashamed to yell. Smart people carry whistles for just such an occasion.

If you can retrace your steps with certainty to the last place where you knew your location (or, if you have become separated, the last place you saw your group), then do so. Use sticks or rocks to make arrows on the trail showing the direction that you are traveling. Otherwise, sit tight until you have a plan or until a third party is able to locate you.

If your entire party gets lost near dark, stop, set camp, and rest. The morning sun can go a long way toward reorientation. In hot climates, travel only during the early morning or late afternoon. In cold climates, if you are without camping gear, you may need to sleep during the day. Stay hydrated. Although it may be unpleasant, most healthy people can go at least a week without food, so make water your first priority.

In a situation where your party is lost for an extended period of time, you may need to search away from your camp to see if you can get your bearings. Send parties of two or more people, if possible. Mark trees, use flagging tape, or build rock cairns so that you can retrace your steps back to your camp. Prioritize safety above Leave No Trace concerns.

Searching for a Lost Person

You can avoid having to search for a lost person by having your group agree to stay within sight of each other while you are moving. Clear camp boundaries, and a designated general area for bathroom use, make it less likely that someone will wander too far from camp and get lost. If, however, someone from your group gets separated, use the following steps to help locate them.

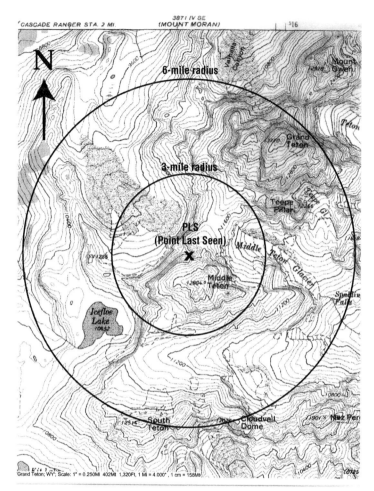

"Point Last Seen" circles help focus the search for a lost person.

Immediately give a few quick shouts, and pause to listen for a response. Often, this is all that is required to locate someone. If you get no response, mark the spot on the map where the person or group was last seen—the Point Last Seen (PLS). If the PLS is close (less than a quarter mile), immediately head to that spot, yelling or whistling every minute or so. Otherwise, draw two circles, one with a 3-mile radius around the PLS and the other with a 6-mile radius. Half of all lost people are found within the first circle; a full 90 percent are found within the second. Focus your efforts within the first circle, and then the second one, keeping the following suggestions in mind:

- Set up an area of confinement that boxes in the lost person by leaving notes, sleeping bags, or other signals in likely traffic areas, such as trail intersections and trailheads. Confine quickly and farther than you suspect the lost person may have gone.
- Determine the urgency of the situation by considering the lost person's age, mental state, wilderness skill level, clothing, food, gear, special medical concerns, weather, and terrain, as well as your own intuition.
- Identify likely areas that the separated person might be, and mark those on the map. Could they be looking for water? Trying to photograph something? Fishing? Did they make a wrong turn at a recent trail intersection?
- In an area where an accident is possible (places with steep rocks, river crossings, or other hazards), search potential accident sites first.
- Look downhill. Rarely do lost people stray uphill.
- If you have a large group, break into search teams and set specific meeting times and locations for reuniting. Send one team to the PLS and the rest to other likely areas.
- Have teams travel light and look for clues, as well as the missing person.
- Don't search at night unless there is a true emergency. It is very strenuous and significantly less efficient.

You may use the method of drawing a circle to help you locate yourself if you become lost. Instead of using a PLS, draw a circle around your last known point. How long have you traveled since you were there? The distance you can travel in that time should be the radius of your circle. Have you been going uphill or downhill? In one continuous direction or meandering? What land features can you see that match those in the circle? In North America, if you are long overdue, a search and rescue (SAR) team will be activated. An air search is likely if the weather permits—planes and helicopters will not fly in bad weather, and they generally will not fly at night.

If you are resigned to sitting still and waiting to be rescued, here are some things you should know:

- Big searches in wilderness areas can take days. You will need food, water, and shelter. Stay organized, and plan how you will conserve resources and stay alive during this period.
- Camp in a visible area—the more open, the better. Try to get to a spot that is easily seen from above.
- Large, smoky fires are visible from great distances. Build one and keep it going; however, don't make a bad problem worse by letting it get out of control. Make it visible, but keep it controlled. Build it in the open and away from trees.
- Carry signal mirrors, and know how to use them before you need them in an emergency. Get out in the open, and have them ready to use before you hear air traffic. SAR pilots say signal mirrors are the single most effective visual aid for identifying lost parties on the ground.
- Geometric patterns are often visible from the air. Triangles, squares, or circles made with rocks, branches, dirt, or extra gear may help. Brightly colored clothing and gear will also help to get you noticed—blues and reds are the most likely colors to attract a pilot's attention.

Emergency Beacons

The technology available to backcountry travelers allows for remarkable communication from remote wilderness locations. At the press of a button, handheld emergency beacons can send out a distress signal from virtually anywhere on the planet. This is, of course, very helpful in an emergency, but there are downsides as well. As these beacons have penetrated the recreational market, the rate of false alarms has increased tremendously. False alarms are an enormous waste of resources, and can be dangerous for those responding to an emergency beacon. If you choose to use such a device in your backcountry travels, you owe it to your potential rescuers to use it responsibly. Emergency beacons should never be used in a location where conventional frontcountry EMS services can be summoned by phone.

The satellite-linked gadgets available on the market today are based on one of two kinds of technology: locator beacon and global satellite communicator.

A locator beacon is a smaller-scale version of the same sort of homing beacons found in aircraft and ships. There are three types of beacons used to transmit distress signals: EPIRBs (Emergency Position Indicating Radio Beacon)—maritime, ELTs (Emergency Locator Transmitter)—aviation, and PLBs (Personal Locator Beacon)—handheld personal units. This technology was originally intended for emergency transmissions only, and operates independently of other means of communication. A modern PLB is GPS-enabled and, when activated, includes your location with its automated transmission. The emergency transmission is relayed to a network of satellites named COSPAS-SARSAT. The satellites relay information about your PLB (its unique serial number, etc.) and its GPS coordinates to a control center, which then involves appropriate local resources to effect a rescue. The PLB system monitored by COSPAS-SARSAT is designed specifically for emergency response. It has limited features, but is very reliable. A PLB does not provide nuanced communication, nor does it offer two-way communication. It merely sends a simple "help" message, with the assumption that the situation is a life-or-limb emergency.

Satellite communicators have been in commercial use since SPOT first introduced them in 2007. They do not use the COSPAS-SARSAT satellite constellation, but instead operate through the commercial satellite constellations used by satellite phone service providers, such as Globalstar and Iridium. SPOT, and more recently inReach, have brought what used to be exclusively high-end and expensive technology into the reach of backcountry travelers. Satellite communicators are more flexible; inReach, for example, can be paired with a smartphone for sending and receiving SMS text messages via the satellite. If you need help, but perhaps do not need helicopters and a platoon of SAR operators, a message directed to a responsible friend in the frontcountry may give you a more appropriate response.

PLBS VERSUS SATELLITE COMMUNICATORS

If you have decided to purchase an emergency beacon, you need to decide whether to buy a PLB or a satellite communicator. Most PLBs serve a critical, but mostly singular, purpose: They tell search and rescue that you need assistance at your location. Satellite communicators do that too, but they can also perform a variety of other communication functions, such as sending short emails or texts and sending friends or family your coordinates so that they can track your progress or come to your assistance without involving SAR.

Why would anyone pick a PLB and give up the extra features of a satellite communicator? The three main reasons are long-term cost, reliability, and simplicity of use.

- **Cost:** PLBs are initially more expensive, but they do not require a subscription service. Satellite communicators often require a monthly fee to activate their services. If you plan to use the service for more than a couple of years, you would save money in the long run by carrying a PLB instead. Costs and service plans are constantly changing. Do your research to see if the monthly service plan can be suspended, what termination fees may apply, etc.

- **Reliability:** The strength of the PLB broadcast signal (4 to 5 watts) is at least ten times more powerful than satellite communicator signals. This makes PLBs slightly more effective, particularly in dense tree cover and bad weather. The dedicated COSPAS-SARSAT system for monitoring PLBs has been in use for marine and aviation emergencies since 1984. Since that system is managed and used by government agencies from many nations, it is likely to be well-maintained and reliable for decades to come.

- **Simplicity of use:** Some satellite communicators can pair with smartphones, but the pairing process and need to decode blinking lights on the devices leaves room for operator error—not ideal in a time of crisis. PLBs have few operator controls and are specifically designed to allow for easy operation.

Conclusion

Knowing how to take care of yourself, and having the ability to avoid getting lost, is far more important than what gadgets you have in your pack. Reduce the consequences of getting lost while you are learning to navigate by keeping your trips short and visiting areas where the risks of weather, large predators, and dangerous terrain are minimal. Become comfortable navigating with map and compass, without the aid of landmarks, before heading out on a long off-trail trek.

Remember that if you activate an emergency beacon, you are asking people (oftentimes volunteers) to drop what they are doing and put themselves at risk for you. Before you press that button, or make that phone call, be sure your emergency is worthy of their risk.

CHAPTER 10 | COMPETITIVE NAVIGATION

U nless you are a wilderness instructor or are in the military, you will have to seek out ways on your own to test and improve your navigation skills. Whether you are competitive by nature or just want to sharpen your eye for maps, there are a number of competitions that may suit your navigation needs. Many of these competitions are designed specifically for those who are relatively new to backcountry travel. Competitions needn't be about winning ribbons or medals. Think of the events described here as an organized way to compete against yourself and measure your improvement. Competitions provide a fantastic opportunity to meet folks with similar interests, as well as to learn from experts. Where else can you run through woods at night and get occasional hot meals, meet with support crews, and have medics standing by to help in case of an emergency?

Three of the most popular navigation-based sports to consider are orienteering, rogaining, and adventure racing. If you want to try all three, take them in that order. An ideal progression is to attend some orienteering meets before attempting a rogaine, and then trying a twenty-four-hour rogaine or two before navigating a multiday adventure race.

Your goal for your first orienteering meet or rogaine might simply be to get off the start line. Finishing one of these events is quite an accomplishment. You should "race to finish" for several races before thinking about improving your placement against others. Your first year, in fact, should not be focused on what place you finish, but on learning, meeting people, and having fun.

Orienteering

Orienteering is the sport of cross-country navigation with map and compass. It began as a Scandinavian military exercise in the late nineteenth century and was popularized by the Swedish in Europe. It made its debut in the United States in the 1940s. Today, there are orienteering clubs across the world linked together through the International Orienteering Federation (IOF) and the United States Orienteering Federation (USOF).

Orienteering meets typically feature a number of courses set up for various skill levels. Beginner courses may be only a mile long, while expert courses can be more than 10 miles. Individuals compete by hiking and running through a series of "control points" marked by flags. Competitors start off at different times, following a marked map and description sheet to each point, where there is a special punch to mark the control card, showing that the competitor was there. Selecting the best route between controls is the primary challenge of the sport. The fastest time through the course, with the control card punched correctly, wins.

Orienteering maps are usually 1:10,000 scale and have more detail than typical topo maps. They are set to magnetic north to remove declination confusion. Many maps include details on the vegetation density to help you plan your route. Different colors are often used for this. For example, yellow may indicate open land, white may mean a forested area that is still runnable, and dark green may indicate terrain that is thick or impassable. First-time competitors need to pay careful attention to the legend on their map and expect some differences from standard topos.

Many competitors become attracted to this sport because it demands mental, as well as physical, endurance. The best orienteers are excellent map readers who can run, not excellent runners still learning to read a map—how fast you run doesn't matter much when you are running in the wrong direction. Experienced, competitive orienteers train by running long distances on- and off-trail. As a beginner, however, you should focus primarily on sharpening your map-reading skills. With the excitement of a meet, your speed will automatically pick up.

Following are a few tips for orienteering:

- Warm up before the start.
- Stay hydrated and well-fed before, during, and after the meet.
- Choose the easiest-to-follow route between controls for your first few meets.
- Start on the easier (white or yellow) courses.
- Try counting paces. Get to know your speed and stride length in different kinds of terrain. Have a system for counting paces by the hundred, and know how many of your paces are in a mile.
- Don't follow other competitors. It's poor etiquette, and besides, they may not be headed the right way.
- Wear light pants or gaiters to protect your legs from brush.

As orienteering—or simply "O"—meets have grown in popularity, so have the variety of formats. Today, there are special orienteering meets for mountain bikers (Bike-O) and cross-country skiers (Ski-O). Some meets are even held at night (Night-O).

To learn more about orienteering meets near you, visit the websites of the International Orienteering Federation and the

US Orienteering Federation. Local orienteering clubs often have websites and email lists with calendars to keep you posted on upcoming events.

Rogaining

ROGAINE is an acronym for "Rugged Outdoor Group Activity Involving Navigation and Endurance." The sport of rogaining was born in Australia in the mid-1970s. It differs from classic point-to-point orienteering in several critical ways: Rogaines are team events, with two to five people on a team; they last three to twenty-four hours; and the controls—known as checkpoints—have different point values and can be visited in any order.

Because the checkpoints are spread out over longer distances, most rogaines use smaller-scale (1:24,000 or 1:50,000) maps. A central base camp is set up throughout the race where teams can eat, rest, or plan their next moves. Because teams can travel at their own pace and go any distance they choose, virtually anyone of any age can participate.

Teamwork and team strategy play a major role in rogaining. As with adventure racing, team members must work together to set the best pace, plan their route, and support each other throughout the course. A rogaining course is planned so that no team can reach all of the checkpoints in the allotted time. Teams are forced to choose which checkpoints to head for. Deciding whether to aim for more-distant or harder-to-find checkpoints with higher point values, or whether to save the harder checkpoints for daytime hours and focus on easier ones at night, is up to your team. The team also has to choose whether to search through the night or get a few hours of sleep. The clock, however, keeps ticking.

One unique feature of rogaines is that everyone finishes at the same time. This allows all skill levels to mingle, and is particularly nice for those newer to the sport.

Orienteering clubs and meets are a great place to meet future teammates for a rogaine, and most orienteering clubs have rogaines on their calendar. Another source for rogaines is the International Rogaining Federation (IRF).

Following are some tips for rogaining:

- Know your teammate(s). Train together, discuss your goals, and communicate.
- Start with a few shorter races (less than twelve hours) before tackling a twenty-four-hour pain-fest.
- Consider sleeping for several hours during your first twenty-four-hour race. Plan your sleep strategy with your teammate(s).
- Eat the same foods and use the same clothing and gear during the race that you used while training.
- Train at night and in bad weather.

Adventure Racing

Adventure racing is team, multisport, endurance racing that takes place predominantly in backcountry settings. The standard components of an adventure race are mountain biking, paddling, off-trail running or hiking, and ascending or descending fixed ropes. Depending on the location, some races also feature events such as glacier mountaineering, canyoneering, open water swimming, kayaking, caving, horseback riding, diving, skydiving, or sailing. Races vary in length from several hours to several weeks, and cover distances ranging from 5 to 700 miles. They are typically nonstop events where the clock runs continuously, and sleep management is a critical part of team strategy.

For most adventure races, navigation—whether by boat, bike, or foot—is a constant challenge.

In 1989 French journalist and adventurer Gerard Fusil launched the sport of adventure racing with the first annual Raid Gauloises (pronounced "raid gall-wahz"). The first Raid required coed teams of five to traverse the South Island of New Zealand together by foot, bicycle, and boat. It was a huge success and was followed in 1995 by the Eco-Challenge Expedition Race, which popularized the sport in North America and around the world until its final race in 2002. New Zealand's Southern Traverse, China's Mild Seven Outdoor Quest, and the United States' Primal Quest are similar in length (five to fifteen days).

For the less masochistic, shorter outdoor obstacle course races, like the Spartan Race series and the Tough Mudder Race series, offer a similar flavor but without the navigation challenges of true adventure races. The shorter races (three hours to three days) have made adventure racing accessible to recreational athletes wanting to test their navigation skills and endurance; they are also more affordable and less the exclusive domain of marathoners, pro cyclists, and triathletes.

Some tips for adventure racing:

- Know your teammates before you race with them. Train together when you can. Be sure that you all have the same goal. Are you racing to finish, or to win? What if someone becomes injured? How much sleep will you need, and when will you take it? How will finances be split? Take the time to iron out all these details when the team is forming, not on the racecourse.
- Nothing will drain your energy and slow you down like serious disagreements during the race. Avoid them like the plague. When navigation errors are made (and they will be), support the navigator by minimizing the impact of the error and focusing on getting back on track.

- Make sure every person on your team is at least minimally competent in each event of the race. Encourage everyone to be open and honest about personal skills, limits, and fears, both before and during the race. A tone of honest and open communication is critical and starts long before you reach the start line.
- Give some of your pack weight to your teammates when you are struggling, and take their weight when they are struggling. Vigilantly watch for ways to support each other. It is common to hear rogainers and adventure racers say that the team "is only as fast as the slowest person." Smart teams actually race faster than the slowest person could go on their own by encouraging each other and sharing weight.
- Don't waste time in transition (rest) areas. Have your gear organized, and have a time limit planned for every transition.
- Make sure that each person has a role: team captain, lead navigator, timekeeper, health (food/hydration) monitor, and so forth.
- Have more than one competent navigator on the team. Who takes over if the primary navigator becomes ill? Who makes that decision? When?
- Train at night and in bad weather.

CHAPTER 11 | DIGITAL MAPS AND SMARTPHONE APPS

If you wanted to own all of the paper USGS maps for the state of Colorado, you would need to buy several hundred maps. For Alaska, you would need nearly 1,000. You might need an extra room in your house just to store all of your new maps! This is where digital map software can be helpful. With free maps available online, and a variety of quality map programs, going digital is cheap and easy.

Thanks to the newest generation of tablets, smartphones, and handheld GPS units, you can see your exact location displayed on a digital topographic map in real time. With a small, handheld gadget, you can watch your location on a digital map change as you move. For readers who may have grown up with a touchscreen GPS in the family car, this may not seem like an innovation. But it is indeed, and it is changing the way that people are interacting with wildlands.

Handheld computerized navigation technology is evolving at an astounding rate. With widely available technology, GPS units and smartphones can offer an amazing amount of information to help you navigate. Map software does more than just provide electronic versions of paper maps. Technological mapping tools add extra features, customize the map, and provide interactive elements. Map software allows you to seamlessly connect and customize maps, plot and overlay routes, zoom in and out, search for topographic features, create elevation profiles, and upload and download GPS waypoints.

Powerful computational abilities and enhanced sensors in smartphones make it possible to change the way navigators think about their tools. Augmented reality apps are one such advancement. Augmented reality blends data display with a view of the world around you. This is the consumer version of the "heads-up display" previously used only in military vehicles. With augmented reality, you can use your phone as a viewfinder to the landscape. Point it at a peak, and it can augment your view by superimposing the name of the peak, its distance from you, the compass direction, the peak's elevation, and other interesting data.

If you are not computer savvy, the techy gadgets may not be for you. Navigation in the backcountry may include digital tools, but they are certainly not a requirement. This book has tried to emphasize the basics, using simple, reliable tools along with your own skills. You can achieve your backcountry goals without a single digital device. The greatest feats of land-based exploration in world history have had nothing to do with electronics. But if the digital world is your thing, this chapter will point you toward some exciting new ways to increase your navigation speed and accuracy.

A simple paper map, a magnetic compass, and your brain can get you where you need to go in most environments. Electronics can enhance your navigation skills, but should not be used to bypass developing those skills in the first place. Learn to navigate with map and compass first.

Before you dive into the ocean of digital possibilities, take a moment to evaluate why you want to go into the backcountry. Many people do so precisely because that environment provides separation from the "rat race" of digital attachment. Bringing a smartphone, GPS, tablet, etc., into the wilderness can seriously detract from an otherwise empowering and self-reliant trip.

A lot can be learned by being immersed in an environment that is untouched and uncontrolled by human influences. In

Electronic gadgets can be helpful navigation tools, but don't overdo it.

fact, a lot can be learned by being lost in the wilderness and having to find your way out on your own. If you find that digital tools enhance your experience, then by all means use them. However, you should have the skills (and practice) to navigate your way to safety without gadgetry. The power and other limitations of digital tools make them not quite fail-safe for backcountry travel. Thinking about your (or your group's) reasons for wilderness travel will help you decide what to take and what not to take.

Map Software

Not so long ago, map software for wilderness navigation was used only by the military, a few professionals, and a handful of dedicated recreationists. Computerized systems have evolved from being enhanced planning tools (marking up custom maps, overlaying routes, etc.) to being real-time displays of location and environment.

As a planning and exploration tool, computers allow you to connect satellite photos, hillshading, topo maps, and other geographic features. Switching from satellite images to topo lines, particularly in an area you know well, can help you better understand how topo lines take their shape. Nothing beats being in the field and comparing the land features you are seeing to the map you are holding in your hands, but the ability to zoom in and out and scroll through terrain gives you a rough understanding of the scale and complexity of the environment that you will be in. That understanding enhances your ability to accurately plan and follow wilderness routes. For the majority of recreationists, Google Earth is the only map software that they will ever need.

Map software capabilities have miniaturized to fit on smartphones and GPS receivers. Many GPS handhelds come preloaded with topo maps for the country in which they are sold. This can save time and effort, as you don't need to locate and download particular maps. If you are purchasing a handheld, it makes sense to buy one with preloaded maps, which tend to function more seamlessly than standalone or online maps.

Smartphone versus Smart-GPS

GPS units allow for data transfer via a wireless network connection or a cable attached to your computer. You can upload or download waypoints, tracks, routes, or map data. This means that you can plan routes on your computer and then upload them to your GPS. It also gives you the ability to leave your GPS set to track while you are out, and then overlay your tracks onto a digital map when you get back home. You can then compare your map and compass-based location estimates with the GPS data—another great way to build your terrain association skills.

The alternative to standalone GPS handhelds with a map display is a smartphone or tablet computer with GPS capability. Most smartphones have GPS hardware built in. Smartphones and tablets in the wilderness, however, present other challenges:

1. They must be charged regularly.
2. They are more fragile than GPS handhelds and require specialized cases.
3. Some navigation apps will not work without Wi-Fi or a cellular signal.

Unfortunately, many of these smart-GPS models also cost as much as, or more than, a smartphone. So, if you already own a smartphone, why buy a GPS handheld? Most GPS units provide longer battery life while in navigation mode (four to twenty-four hours) than smartphones running navigation apps (one to four hours). Also, you can replace batteries in GPS handhelds in the field. If you don't already own a smartphone, or you don't want to mess with portable power and daily recharging, a smart-GPS unit might be your gadget of choice.

Smartphone Apps as Wilderness Navigation Tools

There are many reasons, aside from navigation or emergency communication, why someone might want to carry a tablet or smartphone into the wilderness. With a growing number of natural history applications (apps) for tablets and smartphones designed for field use (e.g., Audubon guides), carrying a tablet and a solar recharger makes sense.

Apps are computer software that allow you to use the data from your device's hardware. The most powerful apps are able to combine data from this hardware with map data to provide you with stunningly accurate and easy-to-understand navigation information.

If you search for GPS apps on the internet, most of what you will find will be apps based on street atlases for frontcountry use. Some apps are server-based—they require an internet connection to constantly download the appropriate map as you travel. Before you purchase an app, be sure that it provides access to maps suitable for backcountry travel (i.e., topographic maps instead of planimetric maps). Also, ensure that it can operate when its data connection is not active.

Whatever your reasons for owning a tablet or smartphone, it is important to understand a few key things about what they can and cannot do to assist you with wilderness navigation. A tablet computer with GPS hardware can process GPS data and display your location on a screen that is larger than those found on many GPS handhelds. The large touchscreen and high resolution makes it simple to zoom in on otherwise tough-to-read areas of the map. In effect, tablet-size screens make digital map reading in the field easier than reading paper maps. Tablets and smartphones make it simple to quilt together maps to give a better view of zones that straddle two paper maps.

The tradeoffs, however, are significant—the potential to de-train our brains for terrain association and the unending need for recharging the devices are two big disadvantages. Touchscreens don't work well with gloves. Smartphones are not designed for the backcountry user: Their operating conditions are limited. Apple's iPhone and iPad list 10,000 feet (about 3,000 meters) as the maximum operating altitude. Acceptable temperatures for operation are between 32°F (0°C) and 95°F (35°C). Without a protective case, these devices are fragile in rugged backcountry conditions.

Depending on the brand and model of your device, the amount of built-in navigation-related hardware sensors can be astounding. In addition to the digital compass, accelerometer, and integrated GPS, many smartphones now have a barometer and a three-axis gyroscope. The gyroscope can combine data with the accelerometer to provide the gadget with awareness of its speed, distance, and directionality in three-dimensional space. In essence, it can know where it is, which way it is pointing, and which way is up. A few years ago, this kind of technology could only be found on satellites, planes, and rockets.

Augmented Reality Navigation Apps

One exciting development in electronically assisted wilderness navigation is the user interface known as augmented reality (AR). Augmented reality is viewing the real physical world through a live camera image that adds computer-generated sensory input, such as position, heading, speed, distance to destination, or points of interest. AR is what the world looks like from the Terminator's perspective; that is to say, you can see the world around you, but you also have additional information appearing in your field of view.

If you've ever played Pokémon GO, you've used an augmented reality app. This location-based game imposes game elements in the view of the real landscape in which you are traveling. Imagine pointing your phone at a hillside, and instead of revealing fantasy creatures, it overlays the path of the trail on top of your view of the hill. The elevation gain, travel distance, and other navigation data can be laid on top of that. This is the promise of AR for navigation, but as this book goes to press in 2018, the technology is not quite there.

What makes the AR navigation experience so unique is not only the continuous navigation data, but also the way that data is presented. It enables the navigator to "see" their destination, or point of interest, directly through whatever buildings or land features might be in the way. This technology will change the way land navigation is done, particularly in low-visibility emergency situations. If you can "see" your destination through a thick forest of trees by merely panning around with your phone, you can hardly get lost (at least not until the batteries run out, which may not be long).

AR for backcountry pursuits has been in development for some time, and the promise of these tools is exciting to consider. Oakley and RideOn (among others) are building AR into ski goggles, for example. Many augmented reality apps that are available today are games, which is where a lot of the development has been in recent years. Navigation apps are easy to find in your usual app marketplace. Most are free or available in a free trial version.

It's a good idea to download and try out several apps before you really need them. Theodolite Pro (www.hunter .pairsite.com/theodolite) makes you feel like you are in the cockpit of a fighter jet: The display can seem tactical and data-centric. ViewRanger (www.viewranger.com) provides a social media integration to share routes. Its "skyline" feature is a friendly demonstration of AR capabilities. Spyglass (www

Just one example of many apps that can be used in the wilderness

.happymagenta.com/spyglass) is somewhere in the middle. Others are out there; download them, and find the one that suits you.

The crux for AR to be truly revolutionary is the ability to match sensory data about location, direction, orientation, etc., with a database of geographic features. This means that AR apps may have to maintain access to a network connection in order to provide full features, which limits backcountry use. Such data requests are also power-hungry uses of your phone's battery.

Conclusion

There are countless apps that will perform a single navigation function, such as providing a digital compass display, giving your elevation, or tracking your mountain bike ride. Select a few that you like, practice using them regularly, and get to know them well.

When and how you decide to use these powerful new tools is critical. On expeditions, it is smart to save the batteries for emergency use, such as traveling at night or in a blizzard. Even then, you will need a recharge if you plan to use the device the following day. If you are using the device for anything other than navigation or communication, and you are in an area with a weak or nonexistent cellular signal, keep the device powered off or in airplane mode. Constantly searching for a cell signal (even while driving to a trailhead) will kill your device's batteries as quickly as having the camera or GPS running. Understanding how to conserve battery power in your device is as important as understanding how to use it for navigation.

Afterword

With some basic navigation skills and practice, you can get into the backcountry with some confidence. Backcountry experiences have the potential to recharge and invigorate. At NOLS, we believe that visiting wild places can change lives. Getting into wild places is valuable to people for different reasons. In the United States, and in many other places around the world, wild places exist because we collectively decide to preserve them in some way. These lands are available because they have been found to hold value precisely because they are wild or inaccessible.

Most public lands in the United States are managed for multiple uses. Recreational users are both the reason we have these lands and one of the major threats to their continued existence. Public lands in North America, and in many other parts of the world, face ongoing threats, from overdevelopment to overuse. In areas near large population centers, we are loving our public lands to death.

Overuse can be managed a couple of ways: fewer users or lighter usage. "Fewer users" is up to land managers. They set maximum thresholds for the number of visitors based on the observed impact to the land itself. You can help with the "lighter usage" factor by carefully following the Leave No Trace principles (see www.lnt.org). Users must be diligent in caring for these areas, and land managers can restrict or temporarily deny access to these areas so that they can recover. When there's a choice, choose the road less traveled, and avoid crowded, highly impacted areas.

Appendix

Suggested Reading

Burch, David. *Fundamentals of Kayak Navigation*, 4th ed. Falcon, 2016.

Calder, Nigel. *How to Read a Nautical Chart*, 2nd ed. International Marine Publishing, 2012.

Eyges, Leonard. *The Practical Pilot: Coastal Navigation by Eye, Intuition, and Common Sense*. International Marine Publishing Company, 1989.

Harvey, Mark. *The National Outdoor Leadership School's Wilderness Guide*. Simon & Schuster, 1999.

Maloney, Elbert S. *Chapman Piloting & Seamanship*, 68th ed. Hearst Books, 2017.

Marion, Jeffrey. *Leave No Trace in the Outdoors*. Stackpole Books, 2014.

Schimelpfenig, Tod. *NOLS Wilderness Medicine*, 6th ed. Stackpole Books, 2016.

Index

A

adventure racing, 158, 162–64
aiming off, traveling off-trail, 93–94
Alaska, topo maps of, 4–5
alders, walking through, 99
altimeters, 19–20, 107–12
  digital, analog, 109, 110
  GPS-based, 111
  orienting yourself with, 111–12
  See also barometric altimeters
apps (computer software), 170
  augmented reality (AR), 166, 171–73
  conserving battery power in, 174
  limits of, 1
  See also smartphones; Global Positioning System (GPS)
arroyos. *See* drainages
atlases, coordinate systems in, 115–16
  See also maps
attack points, off-trail, 95
  See also route, planning
augmented reality (AR) apps, 171–73
azimuth ring. *See* compasses

B

backcountry experiences, value of, 175
backpacking, ix
backstops, off-trail route, 95, 104
bamboo, walking through, 99
barometers, 108
  on smartphones, 171
  See also barometric altimeters
barometric altimeters, 17, 107, 108–11
  See also altimeters
batteries, x
beacons. *See* emergency beacons; PLB (Personal Locator Beacon)
bearings, 67–78
  back bearings, 75–76
  exercises for, 80–84
  plotting on map, 73–75, 76
  from terrain, 72–73
  and triangulation, 77–78
  See also compasses
bezel. *See* compasses
Big Dipper, 41
blazes, on trees, 90, 91
boulders, 97–98
  boulder fields, 95, 97